Children's Church Sermons
—for—
Worship Service

Preparing the Next Generation

SUNDAY BURGER

CROSSBOOKS

CrossBooks™
A Division of LifeWay
1663 Liberty Drive
Bloomington, IN 47403
www.crossbooks.com
Phone: 1-866-879-0502

Unless otherwise indicated, Scripture quotations are taken from the New Century Version®. Copyright © 2005 by Thomas Nelson, Inc. Used by permission. All rights reserved.

Scripture quotations shown with "NIV" are taken from THE HOLY BIBLE, NEW INTERNATIONAL VERSION®, NIV® Copyright © 1973, 1978, 1984, 2011 by Biblica, Inc.™ Used by permission. All rights reserved worldwide.

First published by CrossBooks 04/07/2014

ISBN: 978-1-4627-2859-6 (sc)
ISBN: 978-1-4627-2861-9 (hc)
ISBN: 978-1-4627-2860-2 (e)

Library of Congress Control Number: 2013910075

Printed in the United States of America.

This book is printed on acid-free paper.

Any people depicted in stock imagery provided by Thinkstock are models, and such images are being used for illustrative purposes only.

Certain stock imagery © Thinkstock.

This book is dedicated to my God, the God of the Holy Bible; and to His Son Jesus Christ, my Lord and Savior, who died on the cross for me; and to His Holy Spirit, who lives in me and comforts and guides me. I also dedicate this book to all children. I have been exceedingly blessed to work with children, see them accept the Lord Jesus as their personal Savior, and watch them develop and grow in their relationship.

Table of Contents

Part III: Summer—June, July, and August

Part IV: Fall—September, October, and November

Part V: Extra Lessons for Months with Five Sundays

Preface

It is for all children that this book was written. I humbly ask God's blessings upon it so it can be used as a resource to disciple the next generation of crusaders in building our Lord's kingdom.

Let us unite and accept the responsibility given to us to teach our children the ways of God. Psalm 119:9 says, "How can a young person live a pure life? By obeying your word." It is our duty to teach our children God's Holy Word. We can no longer be naïve and think our children will automatically accept God and His teachings without our involvement and commitment to them. As with all things with God, there are blessings upon blessings from obedience. Also, when we teach our children about God, we worship God; we honor and glorify Him!

It is my prayer that this book will help you develop and expand your children's ministry during the worship service or any time spent with children. It is written as a teacher's guide. The lessons are structured for a mini sermon lasting between four and six minutes. Each sermon is presented in the form of a script, providing easy reference. You can highlight key words for quick reminders and tailor the lessons to meet the needs of your own children. I encourage you to add your own personal twist on everyday experiences, relax, listen to God's voice, and have fun with the little ones!

Acknowledgments

I want to personally thank my family, friends and heros for always supporting, inspiring, forgiving and loving me.

The Soldiers, Veterans and Patriots; past and present of the United States of America- thank you for committing your life and shedding your blood to defend our freedoms and liberties; I am grateful for everything but especially to be able to write this book and share the Gospel.

Pastor Randy Irons-my former pastor, for first encouraging me toward children's church ministry during the Worship Service in 1995.

Pastor Rick Atkins-my current pastor and friend; thank you for your constant encouragement and dedication to our children. Also my church family at New Providence Missionary Baptist Church- I love you dearly.

Martha Moree, Joyce Duncan and Donna Trentham-my solid gold girlfriends who each have a special place in my heart forever.

Dr. Jessica Smiley-Hedrick-thank you for loving me and taking care of me.

The Murphy Clan- thanks to all my family, especially to my precious Granny Murphy, my sister Ruthie, Aunt Ruth and Aunt JoAnn.

Bill and Jannette Holt-I am forever grateful for my parents, who have always loved me and taught me about Jesus when I was young.

The Burger Clan-special thanks to my wonderful mother-in-law Annette, sisters Christie and Debbie, and their families.

Hannah and Hank-it has been my greatest privilege to be your Mom.

Curt Burger-I love you and I am so blessed you are my husband and friend.

Introduction

This book is a collection of mini sermons, usually five minutes, taught during our worship service on Sunday mornings. I am excited to be apart of New Providence Missionary Baptist Church. Our church has a vision for teaching our children to be disciples of God's Holy Word as well as preparing them to defend their Faith and carry it into the next generation. Our children are the Church's future soldiers in the battle to build God's Kingdom. We must prepare them. This manual will help your Church include children ages 3-11 in the main worship service. It will help teach them foundational doctrines of the Bible; God's love, Jesus' sacrifice on the cross and the comfort and companionship of God's Holy Spirit. It's a guide to help teach your children about Jesus so intimately, they can come to know Him as Lord and Savior. It will build on that commitment and grow their relationship with Jesus based on fundamental foundations in God's Word. Deuteronomy 6:4-9 says, *"⁴Listen, people of Israel! The Lord our God is the only Lord. ⁵Love the Lord your God with all your heart, all your soul, and all your strength. ⁶Always remember these commands I give you today. ⁷Teach them to your children, and talk about them when you sit at home and walk along the road, when you lie down and when you get up."* This book teaches Biblical life lessons that will help you prepare your children for the struggles they will encounter as children, the challenging teenage years and into adulthood. I heard President Ronald Reagan say in a speech one time that when, "we abandon the principles in the Bible, we do so at our own peril." One of the greatest gifts we can give our children is to internalize in them the principles of God's word. One of the greatest gifts we can give our Lord is to invest in His Kingdom. Please join us in raising up the next generation of warriors for our Lord and Savior Jesus Christ.

PART I

WINTER

December, January, and February

Baby Jesus

Scripture: Luke 2:1–14 and Isaiah 53:4–5 (NIV).

Christian Truth: Jesus was born to heal us of our sins by taking our wounds on His body.

Visual Aid: Adhesive bandages and gauze.

Good morning and welcome to God's house. Who has been cut before? How did you get cut? Did it hurt? What did you do to help the cut heal? That's right: you put a bandage or Band-Aid on it. *(Show bandage.)* Anybody ever had a really big cut or wound? Yes, you have to put a bigger bandage on it or maybe some gauze. *(Show gauze.)* What is gauze? That's right: it's strips of cloth to stop bleeding.

Let's read Luke 2:1–14. *(Tell them the reading is extralong but that it is very important to listen to all of it; some kids have never heard the Christmas story.)* Everybody put your hands in your lap and look at me.

> [1]At that time, Augustus Caesar sent an order that all people in the countries under Roman rule must list their names in a register. [2]This was the first registration; it was taken while Quirinius was governor of Syria. [3]And all went to their own towns to be registered. [4]So Joseph left Nazareth, a town in Galilee, and went to the town of Bethlehem in Judea, known

as the town of David. Joseph went there because he was from the family of David. ⁵Joseph registered with Mary, to whom he was engaged and who was pregnant. ⁶While they were in Bethlehem, the time came for Mary to have the baby, ⁷and she gave birth to her first son. Because there were no rooms left in the inn, she wrapped the baby with pieces of cloth and laid him in a box where animals are fed. ⁸That night, some shepherds were in the fields nearby watching their sheep. ⁹Then an angel of the Lord stood before them. The glory of the Lord was shining around them, and they became very frightened. ¹⁰The angel said to them, "Do not be afraid. I am bringing you good news that will be a great joy to all people. ¹¹Today your Savior was born in the town of David. He is Christ, the Lord. ¹²This is how you will know him: You will find a baby wrapped in pieces of cloth and lying in a feed box." ¹³Then a very large group of angels from heaven joined the first angel, praising God and saying: ¹⁴"Give glory to God in heaven, and on earth let there be peace among the people who please God."

What was baby Jesus wrapped in? That's right: swaddling clothes or pieces of cloth, just like our gauze! Why? Actually, it was common to take old clothes and rip them into strips to wrap around the baby. Why do you think God would allow His Son to come to earth and be born without even a blanket and have to be wrapped up in strips of cloth in an old barn?

We have to read Isaiah 53:4–5:

> ⁴But he took our suffering on him and felt our pain for us. We saw his suffering and thought God was punishing him. ⁵But he was wounded for the wrong we did; he was crushed for the evil we did. The punishment, which made us well, was given to him, and we are healed because of his wounds.

Jesus left Heaven to come to earth to be born as a little baby and then grow up and die on the cross to save us from our sins! To do that, Jesus had to take all of our sins in His body. It was very painful and hurt Jesus.

4

Jesus was covered in the worst cuts you can ever have, and He did this because He loves us! So when Jesus was born and wrapped in strips of cloth, He was really wrapped in bandages! That was His whole purpose in coming to earth.

Thank you, Lord Jesus, for being wounded for us and taking away our sins! That is what Christmas is really about!

Who wants to pray today? *(If you have a microphone, assist the child in using it.)*

The Legend of the Candy Cane

Scripture: Isaiah 1:18.

Christian Truth: Everything about Christmas is all about Jesus.

Visual Aid: Candy cane to show, candy canes for the children, and miniature candy canes with "Isaiah 1:18" on a label for the children to pass out to the congregation. (You might need the youth group to help, or you might just put the basket at the exit for folks to pick up on their way out.)

Good morning and welcome to God's house. How are you? I am glad you are here! Christmas is coming soon, and I want to talk about my favorite Christmas candy: the candy cane!

Who likes to lick on candy canes? Yes, I think everyone does! Did you know that legend says that a long time ago in Germany a choirmaster (just like Trey, who leads our choir at church) was putting on a Christmas program? The choirmaster couldn't get the little kids to be quiet and listen. He decided to go to the local candy maker, because little kids love candy. He asked the candy maker to make some candy shaped like the shepherd's staff so the little kids would have something to occupy themselves and hopefully keep them quiet.

Why do you think the German choirmaster wanted it shaped like a shepherd's staff? *(Hold up a candy cane each time you ask a question about it.)* Yes! Because when Jesus was born, the angels went to tell the shepherds who were out watching their sheep that the Savior was born and that they should go see the baby!

Later on, around the year 1900, a Christian candy maker in Indiana in the United States decided to add peppermint and to add three small stripes and one big one. Why do you think the Indiana candy maker added delicious peppermint? These are all good answers. Yes, it does taste yummy, but it was because the peppermint plant is in the hyssop family, and it is used for cleansing. What did the baby Jesus being born have to do with getting clean? That's right: the baby Jesus grew up and then died on the cross to save us from our sins, and He washed our sins away! Hallelujah! Praise the King of Kings!

What do you think the three thin stripes have to do with Jesus? Yes, they represent the Trinity: God the Father, God the Son, and God the Holy Spirit. The candy maker also made the stripes thin and put them close together to remind us of the stripes Jesus suffered on the cross.

What do you think the big red stripe is for? You're right! It is to remind us of the blood that Jesus bled when He was crucified on the cross for us. So red is for the blood, but what is the white for? It goes back to the peppermint. Yes, after Jesus died on the cross and rose the third day for everyone, He offered us a gift. If we confess our sins to Him, believe He died for us, and commit our lives to Jesus as our Savior; He will wash our sins away forever!

Let's read Isaiah 1:18:

> [18]The Lord says, come let us talk about these things. Though your sins are scarlet *(also say, "that means red")*, they can be white as snow.

So the white on the candy cane is for forgiveness! The white is for purity or our sinless lives in Jesus Christ. Because Jesus is perfect and holy, we become perfect and holy and acceptable before God. Yes, everything about the candy cane and Christmas is about Jesus! *(Turn the candy cane upside down.)* J is for Jesus!

Who wants to pray today?

The Nativity

Scripture: Luke 2:8–12 (NIV).

Christian Truth: Jesus was born to save all people.

Visual Aid: Toy castle or white house and/or nativity shed.

Good morning and welcome to God's house! Has anyone ever been to the White House in Washington, DC, or even a palace or castle? You have? It's exciting and different from other houses, isn't it? Our family went to Washington, DC, on vacation, and soldiers wouldn't let us into the White House because we didn't have an invitation or special ticket. They said a very important person lives there, and we could not just show up and go inside.

Do you know who lives in the White House? That's right: the president of the United States. Presidents are very important people, and a regular person can't just stop by and visit the man or woman who is the president. The White House is a big, fancy mansion. They have soldiers guarding the entrances all around it and even up on the roof! There are also high fences all around it. Do you think this works to keep people out? It sure does! This is an important way to keep the president and his or her family safe.

Who knows where Jesus was born? That's right: in a stable or barn. Some people think it might have even been a cave. Are barns or caves fancy? Not at all—and they're definitely no place for a mom to be having a baby. What is a barn for? Yes, that is where animals live but not people. Did God have any soldiers guarding the barn? No, everyone who wanted to visit just came in and visited.

Why do you think God in Heaven had baby Jesus born in a barn? Why didn't God have Jesus born in a big, fancy palace or mansion somewhere with guards?

Let's read Luke 2:8–12:

> 8And there were shepherds living out in the fields nearby, keeping watch over their flocks at night. 9An angel of the Lord appeared to them, and the glory of the Lord shone around them, and they were terrified. 10But the angel said to them, "Do not be afraid. I bring good news of great joy that will be for all the people. 11Today in the town of David a Savior has been born to you; he is Christ the Lord. 12This will be a sign to you: You will find a baby wrapped in cloths and lying in a manger."

Since Jesus came to save all people, would it be easier to get to visit Him in a guarded palace or in a barn? Of course, it would be easier in the barn. Everything about Jesus is easy. Jesus says for anyone and everyone to "come unto me." Jesus was born in a place where everyone was welcome. Jesus wants us to know this and share it with everyone. Jesus came to save all people! Who wants to pray?

The Bible–God's Holy Word

Scripture: Psalm 119:9–11.

Christian Truth: God wants us to read and live by the Bible.

Visual Aid: Instruction manual.

Good morning and welcome to God's house! How are you today? Did everyone have an exciting Christmas? Did anyone get a new toy? I am guessing you all did! Did anyone get a new toy that had to be put together? What is the little book called that comes with the new toy that tells your mom or dad how to put it together? That's right: the instruction manual. When you don't know what to do, you can look at it, and it tells you everything. Maybe you got an instruction manual with a new game and it tells you how to play. The instruction manual has all the rules in it.

Why do the people who sell the new toys and games include an instruction manual? That's right: to help you so you don't have to guess. If you don't know how to play something and no one picks up the instructions and reads them, will you know what to do? Of course not—you have to read the directions!

Who else helps us with instructions? Do your parents and teachers give instructions on how to do different things? Yes, they do every day. Does anyone play sports? Your coaches give instructions on how to play so you can do your best and win games.

How about God—does He give us instructions on how He wants us to live? Absolutely He does! Does God have an instruction manual? Yes, He does! What is the book called in which God wrote down all His instructions for His children to live by? That's right: the Bible!

Let's read Psalm 119:9–11:

> ⁹How can a young person live a pure life? By obeying your word. ¹⁰With all my heart I try to obey you. Don't let me break your commands. ¹¹I have taken your words to heart so I would not sin against you.

The Bible is our instruction book—the Christian's instruction book! God wrote down everything He wants us to do and how to do it. We don't have to guess about what to do about anything.

What if we don't read our Bible? That's right: we will not know God's instructions for us to live holy lives. We have to read our Bible every day! We have to get instructions every day. Who wants to pray today?

New Year's Day

Scripture: Ephesians 4:2.

Christian Truth: God wants us to be patient with others.

Visual Aid: A calendar.

Good morning and welcome to God's house! We had another holiday this week. Who knows what the whole world celebrated this week? That's right: it was New Year's Day! What is New Year's Day? Yes, it's where the old year ends and the New Year starts. We have twelve months that make a year, and then we start all over again counting twelve more to make another year. Last year was 2013, and this year is two thousand and what? That's right: 2014! We have a fresh New Year and a fresh, new start.

What do you think would be a good way to start the New Year? I think the best way is something that honors God. Can you think of some things we can do to honor God or please God? Yes, sharing, telling the truth, and helping are all wonderful. What about being patient with other people? That's no fun! Do you think God wants us to be patient with others?

Let's read Ephesians 4:2:

²Always be humble, gentle, and patient, accepting each other in love.

This part of the Bible was originally written in the Greek language, and in Greek the meaning of *patient* is "slow to boil." What do you think that means? When your mom puts water on to boil to make mac and cheese, what does she do to the stove? That's right: she turns up the heat. When the water gets hotter and hotter, what happens? It starts to boil. That means it's really hot. God doesn't want us to get so impatient or mad at each other that we boil with anger. So to be patient, we must stay calm.

If someone doesn't do what we want right then, what should we do? That's right: wait calmly and patiently. We can choose to stay calm. We can choose to not get mad and irritated. We can take a deep breath and wait a few minutes before we say something we shouldn't. We can think about Jesus and how patient He is with us. Also, we can stop and think about how Jesus wants us to act.

We have a brand-new year ahead of us, and it will please God and make life so much more pleasant if we can be patient and slow to boil with others. This honors God and gets us started out on the right foot! Who wants to pray today?

Cabin Fever

Scripture: Colossians 3:13

Christian Truth: Jesus wants us to get along with everyone.

Good morning, and welcome to God's house. It's cold and miserable outside, and we are cooped up and can't play outside! That's called cabin fever. We get antsy and a little grouchy. We may even start to get impatient and make bad choices.

What are some things that we might start doing? That's right: not sharing, not taking turns, and not helping. What about grouching or snapping at someone? Then what happens? You get mad, the other kid gets mad, and everyone is grouchy and mad. Oh my!

God doesn't want us mad at each other. We might get mad for a minute, but what should we do to make God smile and bring Him glory? That's right: we need to forgive the other person. God doesn't want us walking around in a bad mood. Jesus died for our sins and forgave us so we could live forever with Him in Heaven. Likewise, we need to forgive others when they make us mad. We need to get back to being glad!

Show me: what does your face look like when you are mad? It looks scrunched up. And how do you feel when you are mad? That's right: you feel yucky on the inside. It makes us a mess.

Let's read Colossians 3:13. Everybody put your hands in your lap and look at me with listening eyes.

> [13]Get along with each other, and forgive each other. If someone does wrong to you, forgive that person because the Lord forgave you.

Is that true? Did Jesus forgive us for all our sins when He died on the cross? Yes, He did! So we must forgive everyone everything too! If we don't, the bad, mad feelings poison us and make us cranky and grouchy like them. Who wants to be cranky? Nobody does. Who wants to be like Jesus and love and forgive everyone? We do! That means not being mad anymore. It means forgetting about the whole thing, right? Right! Who wants to pray today?

Winter Mud

Scripture: Isaiah 1:18.

Christian Truth: Jesus died on the cross to cover our sins because we can't do it ourselves.

Optional Object: Clean, white T-shirt and muddy, dirty T-shirt.

Good morning and welcome to God's house! What season is it? That's right: it's winter, and it's cold and wet. When it's rainy, we get mud holes. Who has a mud hole at their house? I sure do. I have a big one in my front yard and an even bigger one down by the pond by our house. Our neighbor has cattle down there, and it is a giant mud hole! Guess what happened when the snow fell yesterday? It covered up the mud completely! I looked and looked, but no mud. It was so beautiful around the pond.

When Hank and Hannah (my kids) were little, they loved to go down to the pond and play in the summertime. They would come back up to the house covered head to toe in mud! They loved to play and get dirty. When they were done, or starting to get hungry, they would head back to the house, knock at the back door, giggle and wait. What were they waiting on? Why didn't they just come in the house? That's right: they knew they couldn't come in. Why? Yes, they were dirty all over. I would have to take the water hose and wash the mud off, and when they were clean, they could come in. That's exactly what Jesus did on the cross for us. We are all sinners; we have all made bad choices and sinned against God.

Pretend you have on white clothes head to toe. Now pretend that every time you sin or do something against God's will, you have to have mud smeared on your white clothes. That's what sin does to our heart and soul. God says that after we reach the end of our lives and we die, we cannot come into His presence in Heaven with sin on our heart. That would be like having muddy clothes instead of clean, white clothes, so we would not be allowed in.

Jesus, however, is perfect and has never sinned, so He volunteered to die for all our sins. That way, we could have clean hearts in front of God when we die. Jesus was our only hope. If you accept Jesus into your heart as Lord and Savior, He washes our heart and soul sparkling clean! He makes us holy in God's eyes. God doesn't see our sin when He looks at us—God sees only His Son Jesus. Before the snow, all I could see around the pond was the dirty mud, but after it was all covered with the beautiful white snow. And when we accept Jesus, we aren't covered with dirty sin anymore but with the blood of Jesus!

Let's read Isaiah 1:18:

> The Lord says, "Come, let us talk about these things. Though your sins are like scarlet, they can be as white as snow."

We thank you, Jesus, for dying on the cross for our sins and washing our sins away. Who wants to pray today?

Water—Solid, Liquid, and Gas

Scripture: Matthew 3:16–17.

Christian Truth: God is three persons: God the Father, God the Son, and God the Holy Spirit.

Visual Aid: Water, ice, and steam.

Good morning and welcome to God's house. Who loves winter? I do most of the time, especially when we get snow! Who played in the snow this week? Wasn't it lovely and fun! Who built a snowman? You did? The sun popped out yesterday. Who still has their snowman? What happened to it? That's right: it melted. How come? What is snow? That's right: it's frozen water. When rain freezes in the sky, it falls down as snow. Then, when it warms back up on the ground, it melts and turns back into water. Then the water fills up the mud holes, usually under the swing sets. Then where does the water go? Some goes down in the ground and some turns into a gas and evaporates. That's where the sun heats it and pulls it up into the sky to make clouds, and then the water falls as rain again. Anybody know what that cycle is called? Yes, that's the water cycle!

Water has three forms; it can be liquid and wet, or frozen like ice and snow, or heated up into a vapor like steam. No matter what form water is in, it's still two parts hydrogen and one part oxygen; we call it H_2O

for short. Hydrogen and oxygen are elements God made, and when He put them together, it made water.

Water is always the same no matter what form it is in. When water is liquid, it's still H_2O. When water is frozen, it's still H_2O. Guess what water still is when it's heated up into a gas? Yes, it's H_2O. When water is ice, is it still water? Yes, the molecules don't change. When water is steamed up, is it still water? Yes, again the molecules don't change. Water can be a liquid, a solid, or a gas, and it's still made up of the exact same molecules of hydrogen and oxygen all the time.

God made water, and water has qualities of God. Water is always H_2O—no matter if it's water, ice, or steam. Our Heavenly Father is God, His Son Jesus is Jesus Christ and God the Son, and the Holy Spirit is the Spirit of God, who lives in us and still is God all at the same time—just like H_2O in water is always the same whether it's in the form of a liquid, ice or steam. God, Jesus, and the Holy Spirit are three different persons of God, just like water, ice, and steam are three different forms of water. God the Father, Jesus, and the Holy Spirit are all God all at the same time.

Everyone here knows my son Hank and his dad Curt Burger and Curt's dad Dean Burger. They are all different people and at the same time all Burgers. That's the way it is with God the Father, God the Son, Jesus, and God the Holy Spirit. They are all different and at the same time all God.

Let's read Matthew 3:16–17:

> [16]As soon as Jesus was baptized, he came up out of the water. Then heaven opened, and He saw God's Spirit coming down on Him like a dove. [17]And a voice from heaven said, "This is My Son, whom I love, and I am very pleased with Him."

It is interesting that the first mention of the three persons of the Trinity—God the Father, God the Son, and God the Holy Spirit—was at Jesus' baptism using water! We serve a great God! Who wants to pray today?

Really Real

Scripture: 1 John 3:16–18.

Christian Truth: The evidence of true love from God is in our actions.

Visual Aid: Chef hat, spoon, and pot.

Good morning and welcome to God's house. It's February, and February is the month of love! Let's talk about how we know whether we have the love of God in our heart.

I have a chef hat, spoon, and pot. Does that make me a chef? No—why? That's right: I have to first use it to cook food—then it makes me a chef. What if I just wear my chef hat around and carry my spoon and pot but never cook? Yes, I just look like a chef but I am not really a chef.

If I have hundreds of books, but I never read them, am I a reader? No, I have to open the book and read.

What if I put on a firefighter's hat and gloves and I ride around in a fire truck but never help put out fires—am I a real firefighter? No, I just look like one.

What if I put on my best clothes, and brush my teeth, and get my Bible and head to church and sing and come home—does that mean I have real love in my heart for Jesus? No, it just means I look like I do. How do you know if you have real, Godly love in your heart?

Let's read 1 John 3:16–18:

> [16]This is how we know what real love is: Jesus gave his life for us. So we should give our lives for our brothers and sisters. [17]Suppose someone has enough to live and sees a brother or sister in need, but does not help. Then God's love is not living in that person. [18]My children, we should love people not only with words and talk, but also by our actions and true caring.

God says that just *saying* we love others doesn't mean it is true. If we truly love others, we *do something* for others, especially someone in need.

How can we show real love to others? Yes, we can share our stuff, help and work, give money, tell the truth, be patient, smile, forgive, hug, take turns, and talk to each other. We can draw pretty pictures and send cards. So many things! Should we just do this when we feel like it? No—all the time! Should we just do it when we are young? No—even when we are grown-ups! Who wants to pray today?

Valentine's Day

Scripture: 1 John 4:7–8.

Christian Truth: Real love comes only from God.

Visual Aid: Funnel and small, empty pitcher.

Good morning and welcome to God's house! How are you? What happens this week that is fun and exciting? That's right: it's Valentine's Day! What is Valentine's Day? Yes, it is the day we celebrate love. What do we do on Valentine's Day? Yes, we show others how much we love them. We can buy them presents from the store, give flowers, or make them a pretty picture. But what if we want to give them love—where do you get real love? Yes, love comes from our hearts. But how does it get there; who puts it there? Yes, you are right: it only comes from Jesus!

Let's read 1 John 4:7–8:

> [7]Dear friends, we should love each other, because love comes from God. Everyone who loves has become God's child and knows God. [8]Whoever does not love does not know God, because God is love.

So the Bible says love only comes from God. And if we truly are children of God, we know how to love! How do we get to be God's child? That's right: we accept Jesus as God's Son, who died for our sins on the cross; we ask God to forgive us of our sins and we make Jesus the Lord of our life—and then we are saved and become God's child. *(Hold the funnel directly over your head and pretend to pour into the funnel with the pitcher.)* God *then* fills us with His Holy Spirit, who then fills us with God's love! How awesome is that! *Then* we can go out and share God's love with others.

How can we do that? Yes, by sharing, giving, taking turns, helping, using kind words, and telling others about Jesus dying on the cross for our sins—that's what Valentine's Day is all about! Who wants to pray today?

God's Love

Scripture: Ephesians 3:18–20.

Christian Truth: God's love is endless.

Visual Aid: Measuring tape.

Good morning and welcome to God's house! What is something really, really wide? What's something really, really long? What about something really, really high and really, really deep? You're right about all those things. Those are all things we can measure. How can we measure something wide or long or high or deep? Yes, with a measuring tape. But how could we measure something wider than wide, or longer than long, or higher than high, or deeper than deep? Stretch your arms out as wide as you can, now reach up high as far as you can. Now the boys reach up and the girls stretch out wide. What does that make together? Yes! The only way is with the cross!

Let's read in Ephesians 3:18–20 to see what God says:

> [18]And I pray that you and all God's holy people will have the power to understand the greatness of Christ's love—how wide and how long and how high and how deep that love is. [19]Christ's love is greater than anyone can ever know, but I pray that you will be able to know that love. Then you

can be filled with the fullness of God. [20]With God's power working in us, God can do much, much more than anything we can ask or imagine.

God's love is bigger than anything that could ever be measured. His love goes on forever, and it never ends. When we ask Jesus to come into our hearts as our Savior, He lives inside us. We have the power of God's love inside us through the Holy Spirit! God's love is so big and so powerful, and He lives inside us. We can do mighty things to bring God glory with His great love! What are some ways we can share God's big love inside us? Yes, we can pray for others. We can help and give to others, work for others, and give people hugs, kisses, and smiles! Let's pray. Who wants to pray today?

Manners

Scripture: John 13:34–35.

Christian truth: God wants His children to show respect for others.

Good morning and welcome to God's house. All month we have been talking about ways to show God's love to others. What are some ways we have talked about? Yes, patience, forgiveness, joyfulness and smiling, gentleness, and self-control. What do we call all these love behaviors? Yes, they are the fruits of the Spirit!

Today, I want to add one more: kindness. What is kindness? It's being kind. What does that mean—"to be kind to someone"? Yes, it means to show love, but how? What about with manners? Who knows what it means to have good manners? What are some good manners? Yes, saying "excuse me" when you need to get around someone instead of just pushing him or her out of the way. What about saying "excuse me" when you are eating and you burp? That is definitely good manners.

What are some more good manners? Yes, when you say "please" when you want something and "thank you" when someone helps you. What do you say when someone offers you something like broccoli and you don't want any? Yes, that's right: you should say, "No, thank you." You can also take turns at the water fountain or when playing games. What should you do when someone is talking and you want to talk? That's right: wait patiently and don't interrupt.

All of these are great manners, and they show kindness to the other person. When you show kindness to someone, you are also showing that person respect. When you show someone respect, you are showing him or her God's love, and you give God glory!

Let's read John 13:34–35:

> [34]"I give you a new command: Love each other. You must love each other as I have loved you. [35]All people will know that you are my followers *if* you love each other."

Jesus says one way we are known as His children is by loving others, and we can love others by showing them kindness—using good manners! Who wants to pray?

PART II

SPRING

March, April, and May

Green Leaves of Spring

Scripture: Proverbs 11:28.

Christian Truth: God blesses His children when they trust Him.

Visual Aid: Big green leaf and a dead leaf.

Good morning and welcome to God's house! Who has noticed something happening on the trees this week? Yes, they are growing new leaves! What happened to the old leaves? Yes, they turned colors In the fall, died, and fell off. Have you ever looked at a green leaf and a dead leaf? How does the green leaf look? Yes, it's green, healthy, gorgeous, and strong. How does the dying or dead leaf look? Yes, it looks just the opposite. It is brown, unhealthy, brittle and weak. If you were a leaf, which one would you want to be? Of course, we would want to be the strong green leaf!

Let's read in Proverbs 11:28:

> [28]Those who trust in riches will be ruined, but a good person will be healthy like a green leaf.

God is saying don't trust money. Whom should we trust? Yes! We should always trust God to take care of us. God says *if* we always trust Him, we will be healthy and strong and we will prosper like a green leaf. If a leaf is green, that means it is growing strong, and when storms come it can make it safely through. Just like us—if we are trusting God, He will help us through a hard situation. But we have to stay close to God at all times.

What happens to the beautiful green leaf if it doesn't have water every day? That's right: it starts to die and to look like this dead leaf. That's exactly what happens to us spiritually if we aren't watered by Jesus every day. The Bible says Jesus is the living water. We need to talk to Him in prayer every day, all day, and we need to read our Bible and do what God tells us. And we need to go help others and tell them about Jesus.

But when a problem comes along, we need to trust Jesus and believe in our hearts with our actions that God will help us through it. God promises to bless us because of our faith!

Who wants to be a "dead leaf" Christian or a "green leaf" Christian? Green leaf for me too! Let's always trust the Lord with our actions! Who wants to pray today?

Time for Spring

Scripture: Ecclesiastes 3:1.

Christian Truth: Patience.

Good morning and welcome to God's house! Who noticed the trees outside this week? What's going on? Yea! It's springtime! Oh, how wonderful and beautiful it is! Everything has been so drab, brown, and gray all winter. God makes us wait and wait, and one morning He decides to take out His paintbrush and *voila*! Color everywhere!

As soon as the blossoms start popping out, I start watching for the purple blossoms on the redbud trees—they are my favorite! All year these trees are green, and then for a couple of weeks in spring they are gorgeous and bright! They seem to turn overnight. Do you think the purple blossoms get impatient waiting a whole year, every year, until it's their turn to blossom and shine? Probably not. God created them to bloom at just the right time every spring, and the trees know that. And so they wait patiently until just the right time. That is their job for God—to bloom bright purple every spring.

Do you think the purple trees wish sometimes they could bloom at a different time, maybe mid-winter? No, that's silly; they were made to blossom in spring, and they are happiest doing what God wants when

God wants. Just like the purple tree, God created us with a purpose and a specific time too.

Let's read Ecclesiastes 3:1:

> ¹There is a time for everything, and everything on earth has its special season.

The Bible says there is a time for everything, and that includes us. We have morning time, lunchtime, dinnertime, school time, play time, study time, church time, and bedtime. No matter what time it is, it's always time to do what God wants, when He wants it, and where He wants it, for His glory!

Is there a special time for each of us to be saved? Yes. Just like when God tells everything in creation it's time to bloom or grow, there is a time for us to be saved. God will tell you when the time comes for you to be saved. God's Holy Spirit will whisper in our hearts, and we will know it's time! Who can tell me what that means to be saved? Yes, it means we know we are sinners and God will not let sinners into Heaven. We know and believe Jesus Christ died on the cross for us because we are sinners and he took our sins on His body. If we ask God to forgive us of our sins and ask Jesus to be the Lord of our life, Jesus will save us from a terrible place called Hell. When we die, we will stand before God, without sin and we will be able to spend forever with Jesus in Heaven. Yes, there is a time for everything, and that includes choosing to be saved through Christ's blood on the cross. Who wants to pray today?

Saint Patrick

Scripture: Matthew 6:14–15.

Christian Truth: We must forgive others.

Good morning and welcome to God's house! This week is Saint Patrick's Day. Who knows who Saint Patrick was? Actually, he was a priest, and Saint Patrick's Day in Ireland, where he lived, is a holy day. Patrick wasn't even his original name. He was born Maewyn Succat of Britain in the fifth century (about fifteen hundred years ago). When he joined the Catholic Church, they required him at his baptism to adopt a Christian name, and so he chose Patrick.

When Patrick was a teenager, he was kidnapped from his home and taken to Ireland to serve as a slave herdsman. They forced him to watch over the sheep and lambs. Ireland was a pagan land, or not a Christian land, but while Patrick was there, he still grew stronger in his faith in God. It took him six years to escape and journey by sea back to his home in Britain.

Fifteen years after he escaped, Patrick returned to Ireland on his own, but this time as a servant of Jesus—a missionary. Even though Patrick had been treated badly while he was a slave in Ireland, and the people were really mean to him, he forgave them and wanted to share God's love with them. Patrick even found the same man who had made him a slave and from whom Patrick had escaped, and Patrick gave him some money. That's real forgiveness!

Do you know why Patrick could forgive the mean man for how he treated him and then turn around and show him God's sweet love? Yes, Patrick was saved and had God's love living in him through the Holy Spirit! Jesus died so we could be forgiven for all our sins! Guess what Jesus wants us to do when someone sins against us?

Let's read Matthew 6:14–15:

> [14]Yes, if you forgive others for their sins, your Father in heaven will also forgive you for your sins. [15]But if you don't forgive others, your Father in heaven *will not* forgive your sins.

We celebrate Saint Patrick's Day to honor a Christian who made the choice to forgive people who were mean to him. This makes Jesus smile when we do that as well. The Bible says that *if* we forgive others, then our sins are forgiven too!

What if we don't forgive others? Jesus says He will not forgive us! Ouch! Jesus is speaking to saved children of God. When we ask Jesus to come into our heart as our Savior, because He died for all our sins, we are forgiven of all our sins forever. After we are saved, we still sin and need to ask God to forgive us. When we are saved and we withhold forgiveness from others, Jesus says it is sin. When we are saved and we have the sin of unforgiveness toward others in our heart, it not only hurts the friendship, but also it separates or blocks our fellowship with God. It inhibits or hurts our relationship with God—just as any sin does.

One way we can show others how grateful we are that Christ died to forgive us of all our sins is to turn around and forgive others when they hurt us. This reconciles the friendship or connects us back with our friend. It also restores our relationship and communication with God.

As children of God, what should we always do when we are mad at someone who hurts us? Yes, forgive always! Now, when you celebrate Saint Patrick's Day, you are really celebrating forgiveness of others every time, just like God forgives His children when we ask every time! Who wants to pray to God today?

Jesus Is God

Scripture: John 10:30.

Christian Truth: Jesus is God's Son, and Jesus is God.

Visual Aid: Family picture.

Good morning and welcome to God's house. Who has pets or animals? Our dog Chloe just had puppies! Springtime is so exciting, when all the babies are born!

What are puppies? That's right: they are baby dogs. They are puppies but at the same time, they are still dogs. They are both puppies and dogs at the same time. What about horses? The momma horse has the baby horses. What are baby horses called? Yes, they are foals. Is a foal, even though it's a baby, still a horse? Of course it is. It is a baby and a horse at the same time.

What about people? We have babies too, but they are still people at the same time. You are all kids, but you are all still people at the same time. Why are you still people even though you are little kids too? That's right: your mom and dad are people, so that makes you people! You are all family! Every one of you has a dad, and you are the son or daughter.

Who is Jesus? Yes, He is God's Son, and God is His Dad. Jesus is Jesus, but He is still God too at the same time.

Let's read John 10:30:

> [30]The Father and I are one.

We are all people but at the same time, we are all sons or daughters just like Jesus is God's Son! Jesus is Jesus and at the same time, Jesus is God. Jesus is God's Son, so that makes Him God too at the same time. Whew! I am glad we have that straight! Who wants to pray to God today?

Easter Egg Hunt

Scripture: Matthew 28:1–7.

Christian Truth: Everything in creation tells the Easter Story.

Visual Aid: Plastic Easter egg.

Good morning and welcome to God's house! This is a very special week! Who knows what we are celebrating this week? Yes! It's Easter, the time we celebrate when Jesus died on the cross for our sins and rose on the third day, which is called Easter Sunday.

We are going to celebrate next Saturday with a special event. Does anyone know what we are doing? Yes, we are having an Easter egg hunt! So exciting! Who knows what an Easter egg hunt has to do with Jesus and Easter? We have had Easter egg hunts for hundreds of years and for the same reason we have them today, and that is to celebrate Jesus dying on the cross for us and rising from the dead.

A long time ago, there was a grown-up person who wanted a way to include children in the Easter celebration. Since everyone had chickens, they decided to make a game out of hiding eggs and letting the kids hunt them for fun. Why do you think they chose eggs to hide—why not rocks or pinecones maybe?

Let's read Matthew 28:1–7 and look for clues to why they used eggs:

> ¹The day after the Sabbath day was the first day of the week. At dawn on the first day, Mary Magdalene and another woman named Mary went to look at the **tomb.** ²At that time there was a strong **earthquake**. An angel of the Lord came down from heaven, went to the **tomb**, and **rolled the stone** away from the entrance. Then he sat on the stone. ³He was **shining as bright as lightning**, and his clothes were **white as snow.** ⁴The soldiers guarding the tomb shook with fear because of the angel, and they became like dead men. ⁵The angel said to the women, "Don't be afraid. I know that you are looking for Jesus, who has been crucified. ⁶**He is not here.** He has risen from the dead as He said He would. Come and see the place where His body was. ⁷And **go quickly** and tell His followers, 'Jesus has risen from the dead.'"

Did you hear any clues from the Bible as to how Easter eggs tell the Easter story about Jesus? First, what shape are eggs? Yes, they are round. What covered the tomb? Yes, a large stone, and eggs are shaped like a stone. Also, eggs are curved and roll just like the stone the angel rolled away to open the tomb.

What's inside an egg? Well, a real egg has food, just like inside the tomb where Jesus was. The Bible says Jesus is the Bread of Life.

When you crack open an egg, it breaks into two pieces, and the Bible says that when Jesus died, the rocks broke apart and the temple veil split in two pieces. Have you ever watched a baby chick come out of its shell? It pecks and pushes until the egg splits and cracks open. That's what happened when Jesus came out of the tomb—the earth shook and split open. The Bible also says that when Jesus comes back, the graves will all open up and the saints will burst out, just like the baby chick comes out of the egg. And when Jesus came out, that left the tomb empty! When you crack open an Easter egg, even the plastic ones, and take out the candy, it's empty just like the tomb.

When a baby chick is hatched from an egg, is it new or old? Yes, they are brand-new baby chicks. When we accept Jesus as our Savior, we become a new creature in Christ. We can have new spiritual life in Jesus.

What color is an egg? Yes, it's white, and the Bible says because Jesus was raised from the dead—and if you are saved—your sins are washed white as snow, just like the color of an egg!

It's very easy to see why we use eggs to celebrate Easter. Which of you are coming to the Easter egg hunt to celebrate Jesus rising from the dead? Wonderful! Who wants to pray today?

Easter Sunday

Scripture: 1 Peter 2:24.

Christian Truth: Easter started at Christmas.

Visual Aid: Christmas ornament or Christmas stocking.

Good morning and welcome to God's house. What is today? Yes, it's Easter Sunday! I know it's Easter—so why would I bring a Christmas ornament to church with me? What does Easter have to do with Christmas? I want you to think back to Christmas, when we read in the Bible that Mary wrapped the baby in "swaddling clothes." Who remembers what swaddling clothes means? Yes, that means that baby Jesus was wrapped in strips of cloth really tight, like a big bandage. Back then, they didn't always have blankets like we do, so they would take scraps of cloth and wrap the baby.

Today is the day we celebrate when Jesus died on the cross on Friday and rose from the dead on Sunday. After the earthquake, the angel rolled the stone away from the entrance to the tomb, and Mary Magdalene and the other women went into the tomb to look for Jesus—but they didn't find Him. When they looked in the tomb, guess what they did find? Yes, all the clothes and bandages that had been wrapped around Jesus for His burial. Jesus had risen from the dead, and He left in the tomb the neatly folded cloth strips. He had risen from the dead and was not there!

We must remember that Easter started at Christmas when Jesus was born. He left His throne in heaven to come to earth. It's important to understand that Jesus was wrapped in bandages as a baby because He would grow up and volunteer to die on the cross for our sins so we could be saved. Jesus knew there had to be a perfect sacrifice for our sins in order for us to be made holy before God. When Jesus was born, He put on the bandages; at Easter, He took off the bandages for us.

Let's read 1 Peter 2:24:

> [24]Christ carried ours sins in his body on the cross so we would stop living for sin and start living for what is right. And you are healed because of his wounds.

The Bible is very clear. Jesus bled on the cross for our sins so our hearts would be healed and made holy before God. Why did Jesus do that? Yes, only one reason—because He loves us! Do we love Jesus? Yes, we do. Thank Jesus today for bleeding and dying on the cross for us! Who wants to pray?

The Dark

Scripture: Ephesians 5:8, 16–17.

Christian Truth: We, as God's children, should shine the light of God's love.

Visual Aid: Flashlight with batteries.

Good morning and welcome to God's house. Who is afraid of the dark? Me too! What do we use when it's dark? Yes, we flip on the lights, lamps, and nightlights to see. What can we use if we are outside or maybe camping? Yes, a flashlight helps us see where we are going. What makes the flashlight work? Yes, the batteries. The batteries are the power source that makes it work and helps it shine.

What if the flashlight isn't working—what do you do? Yes, you put new batteries in it. What if after you put the new batteries in, the flashlight still refused to shine? What if the flashlight said it didn't feel like shining? What if it said it wanted to take the day off from shining? What if it said it was afraid it wouldn't be good at shining and said it just wasn't even going to try to shine? That's crazy! Flashlights were made to shine light into the darkness!

Christians are just like flashlights. We were made to shine God's light. When we get saved, we ask Jesus to come into our hearts, and we become a brand-new creature—we have a new power inside us. Just like a flashlight that has dead batteries, we too are dead and dark on the inside, but when Jesus comes into our heart, He gives us the Holy Spirit, who lights us up with God's love. Just like the flashlight, we are born with the purpose of shining the light inside us on others. This light is God's love.

Let's read Ephesians 5:8:

> [8]In the past you were full of darkness, but now you are full of light in the Lord. So live like children who belong to the light.

In the book of John, it says Jesus is the light of the world, and so we should shine for Jesus! How are we going to shine for Jesus? Yes, we are going to share, help, smile, take turns, and be patient. We are going to give to people in need and tell others about Jesus who died for us.

Ephesians 5:16–17 says this:

> [16]Use every chance you have for doing good, because these are evil times. [17]So do not be foolish but learn what the Lord wants you to do.

So, if we are born-again, new creatures with the love of God inside us, the Bible says we should shine the love light inside us on others who have dark hearts. That way, they can come to know Jesus, be saved, and live with us and Jesus forever! We can do that, right? Yes, we can, because we love Jesus! Who wants to pray today?

Sand

Scripture: Psalm 139:17–18.

Christian Truth: God is always thinking about us.

Visual Aid: Clear jar filled with sand.

Good morning and welcome to God's house. How are you? I am so excited that it is springtime. Every spring, my son Hank and I go buy fresh sand for his sandbox. Who loves to play in the sand? Yes, it feels so good between our toes. It's cool and wet and squishy. I brought some sand today. How many pieces of sand do you think are in this jar? How about in a child's sandbox? How about in our town, Tellico Plains? How about on all the beaches in the world? How about in the whole world? Wow! There are so many pieces of sand that they are impossible for us to count! Do you believe the Bible is God's Word?

Let's read Psalm 139:17–18:

> [17]God, your thoughts are precious to me. They are so many!
> [18]If I could count them, they would be more than all the grains of sand.

Wow! The Bible says that God thinks about us more times than there are grains of sand. That is more than we can even count. God loves us, and He is always thinking about us. He thinks about what we are doing and what we are going to be doing. He thinks about what interests us, scares us, and makes us happy, sad, and afraid. God thinks about us and everything that we think about. We can talk to God about anything. God has a plan for us. He wants to help us. God is our best friend always. He loves us so much and thinks so much about us that He sent His Son Jesus to die for us!

We are important to God. We are God's children. Just like your mom and dad think about you all the time, so does God! Who wants to pray to God today?

Homecoming

Scripture: 1 Thessalonians 4:15–18.

Christian Truth: Jesus is coming back to earth to take Christians to Heaven with Him!

Good morning and welcome to God's house! Today is a special Sunday; does anyone know what today is? Yes, today is Homecoming at our church! What is Homecoming? It's when a lot of people from our church community meet together for a big reunion. Who will be here? Homecoming includes everyone who goes to our church now and everyone who used to go to church (they grew up here maybe and moved away), and the families who have family members buried here in our cemetery—all of these people meet together for a big reunion.

Who has family reunions at home? It's the same thing with our church family. We get together and worship together, fellowship, and visit together, decorate the graves of our family buried here, and then have a big feast!

Did you know that one day soon, Jesus—who is in Heaven right now getting everything ready for us to come to Heaven—is coming back to earth to get all the Christians for a reunion in Heaven?

Let's read 1 Thessalonians 4:15–18:

> [15]What we tell you now is the Lord's own message. We who are living when the Lord comes again will not go before those who have already died. [16]The Lord himself will come down from heaven with a loud command, with the voice of the archangel, and with the trumpet call of God. And those who have died believing in Christ will rise first. [17]After that, we who are still alive will be gathered up with them in the clouds to meet the Lord in the air. And we will be with the Lord forever. [18]So encourage each other with these words.

So just like the whole church got ready today for our reunion here, Christians need to get ready for our reunion with Jesus when He comes back to earth!

How can we be ready? Yes, first we have to be saved. We have to admit we need Jesus as our Savior—that we are sinners and unholy and ask God to forgive us of our sins. We must believe Jesus is God's Son, who died on the cross for our sins and we must commit our life to living for Jesus as our Lord. After we are saved, we will want to be busy telling others about Jesus so they can ask Jesus into their hearts—then we will be ready for our homecoming with Jesus! Who wants to pray?

Mother's Day

Scripture: Ephesians 6:1–3.

Christian Truth: God says to show honor and respect to our moms.

Good morning and welcome to God's house! What is special about today? Yes! It's Mother's Day! What is Mother's Day? It is a special day to show our moms extra honor. What is honor? That's when you treat someone with respect—you show him or her appreciation and love. What is appreciation? That's where we let the special person know how valuable he or she is to us.

Are moms valuable? Yes! What are some things our moms do for us? Yes, she cooks, cleans, takes us places, takes us to church, buys us food and clothes, and reads to us. She also helps us with problems, takes care of us when we are sick, plays with us, and talks to us! Wow! Moms do a lot. How can we honor them today and every day in a way that shows respect, honor, and appreciation?

Let's read Ephesians 6:1–3. (You can ask an older child to read.)

> [1]Children obey your parents as the Lord wants, because this is the right thing to do. [2]The command says, "Honor your father and mother." This is the first command that has a

promise with it— ³"Then everything will be well with you, and you will have a long life on the earth."

So how can we honor Mom, according to the Bible? Yes, we can obey Mom every time, the first time she tells us to do something. This makes God happy when we obey Mom; then as we grow in the Lord, it will be easier for us to obey God.

What else can we do to honor Mom? Yes, we can help her clean the house, carry in groceries, clean up our rooms, and pick up our toys after we play. How about saying "yes, ma'am" and "no, ma'am" when we answer Mom? Also, we should never argue with Mom—just do what she says. Moms are smart. They know things you don't. That's why God gave us a mom to take care of us and teach us the right way to live to bring glory to God! When we honor Mom, we honor God!

Let's really try every day to show Mom respect with the way we act and with the words we say. Who wants to pray today?

School's Out

Scripture: 1 Corinthians 10:31.

Christian Truth: Respecting others with good manners.

Good morning and welcome to God's house. School is out, and summertime fun is officially here. What happens when school's out? We were getting up early, getting ready for school, going to school all day, coming home and doing homework, eating dinner together, taking a bath, and going to bed. Now, we can sleep late—no school, no homework, and no schedule. We start eating dinner at different times, different places. Sometimes we eat at home, sometimes on the go; we may even go on a picnic. Even though our schedules are a little crazy in the summer, it's still really important to sit down and eat dinner together as a family.

Who sits down at the table and eats dinner together most nights? That is excellent! It is so important for families to sit down together to eat. Researchers—that's people who study stuff—they studied kids who sit down and eat dinner together with their family, and they discovered that those kids were less likely to get hooked on drugs and those kids made better grades in school! Usually, this is the only time of day that everyone in the family is together in the same room, and it's a great time to visit and talk and find out what all happened to everyone during the day. So if your family doesn't sit at the table and eat dinner together, I want you to go home and ask Mom and Dad if you can start.

Who knows a good way to eat dinner together? Yes, the first thing is to turn off the TV and then go wash your hands. Ask Mom or Dad—whoever is cooking—if you can help set the table. That means get everyone a plate, fork, spoon, glass, and napkin, and place it at the table. Ask if you can help put food on the table. After everyone sits down—and you need to sit on your bottom on your chair at the table—what should you always do before you eat? Yes, bow your heads and say the blessing. What is the blessing? Yes, that's where we thank God for our food.

After the blessing, we need to fill our plates and always try something new—at least one bite. Always try to eat some vegetables and healthy food. We chew with our mouths closed and never talk while we are chewing. When someone hands you something or asks if you want more, always say please and thank you. Try not to drink a lot at dinner; mostly eat—that way your belly gets full of food. Try drinking water at dinner instead of something with lots of sugar; that way you can start to wind down after dinner and it will be easier for you to go to sleep later. What should you use when you have food on your mouth and fingers? Yes, always use your napkin.

Now when you eat together, everyone needs to sit together until everyone is finished. If you finish first or before everyone else, just sit and wait patiently and join in the conversation.

What is all this behavior called at the dinner table? Very good: it is called good manners. The reason we use good manners is to show other people respect and that they are important to us and we care about them. Why do we do that?

Let's read 1 Corinthians 10:31:

> [31]The answer is, if you eat or drink, or if you do anything, do it all for the glory of God.

So the Bible says, if we eat or drink, or whatever we do, do everything to show others love and respect, and that shows God love and respect! It's a very good feeling when we do the right thing. Who wants to pray to God today?

Summer Schedule

Scripture: Luke 4:16.

Christian Truth: God wants us to read our Bible every day.

Good morning and welcome to God's house! School is out, and everyone is on summer vacation. What are some things you are going to do this summer with all your extra time? I heard someone say go on vacation to the beach, go camping, go swimming, and go fishing. Wow! Sounds like lots of fun things all summer. What are some things you are going to do at home? Yes, some of you are going to ride your bike, play in your tree house, and play with friends.

What do you think Jesus did with His extra time when He was a kid in the summer? He probably did the same things you do: play and have fun. There is something else I think He did, because Jesus did this as a grown-up, and it starts when you are a kid.

Let's read Luke 4:16:

> [16]Jesus traveled to Nazareth, where He had grown up. On the Sabbath day He went to the synagogue, **as He always did, and stood up to read**.

What did the Bible say that Jesus always did? Yes, He always went to church on the Sabbath day, and Jesus always read the Holy Scriptures. Just like Jesus, we need to be reading our Bible daily.

Who is learning to read? Who can read really well? The best way to become a good reader is to read every day. You have to first, *practice*; second, *practice*; and third, *practice*! Every day, I want you to *read by yourself*, and beg someone in your family to read *with you*, and have someone read *to you*. That's three times a day you will be practicing your reading, and really soon you will be a great reader!

There are all kinds of great books that are fun to read. Which book should you read every day? Yes, you should read your Bible every day. The Bible is God's Holy Word. The Bible is a very important way that God speaks to us and teaches us. It is a way we get to know God. The more we read in our Bible, the more we know about our God!

This summer I want you to read, read, read—especially your Bible— every day. You will become more like Jesus! Who wants to pray?

PART III

SUMMER
June, July, and August

Bible School

Scripture: Proverbs 4:25–27.

Christian Truth: The devil wants us to skip Bible school.

Good morning and welcome to God's house! What starts tonight at church? Yes! Bible school starts! I am so excited! It's going to be a rootin' tootin' good time. Bible school this year is set back in the Wild Wild West. It's called Round up for Jesus. Who are we going to round up? Yes, everybody we can find. I want everyone to go home, call all your friends, and invite them. Tell them it starts tonight at six o'clock. Tell them we will have food, crafts, music, and games!

Everyone has been working hard to get everything ready. Do you have to do anything to get ready? What about your heart and your mind?

Guess who really doesn't want you to come to Bible school? Yes, the devil wants you to miss all the fun and excitement, but he especially wants you to miss all the worship and learning about Jesus. The devil doesn't want you to come to Bible school and learn about how much God loves you, or God's forgiveness of our sins, or how Jesus died for our sins on the cross so we can be saved.

The devil doesn't want us to learn about helping people and about Heaven. He wants us to miss all that. Why? Because he doesn't love

God and he doesn't love us. He wants us all to be lost and to stay away from God. He might try to keep us busy so we can't make it to Bible school. Let's decide right now, no matter what, that we are coming to Bible school.

Let's read Proverbs 4:25–27:

> [25]Keep your eyes focused on what is right, and look straight ahead to what is good. [26]Be careful what you do, and always do what is right. [27]Don't turn off the road of goodness; keep away from evil paths.

The Bible says to stay focused on Jesus. That means to always be looking at Jesus, always learning about Jesus, always trying to be like Jesus—and that's exactly what Bible school is all about! Who is coming to Bible school tonight? Hallelujah! Who wants to pray today?

Father's Day

Scripture: Hebrews 12:4–11.

Christian Truth: Godly fathers discipline their children.

Good morning and welcome to God's house! Who knows what special day today is? Yes, it's Father's Day! Today is the day we honor our dads in extra special ways. What are you doing extra special for your dad today? Those are all wonderful ways to show Dad honor and respect. Why do we honor Dad? What has Dad done for you? Yes, he teaches you how to do things; he plays with you; he works hard to buy you food and clothes and take you places! Wow! Our dads do so much for us. We left one thing off the list that great dads do. Any more guesses?

Let's read Hebrews 12:4–11. It's kind of long, so everyone look at me and put your fingers together in your lap—very good.

> ⁴You are struggling against sin, but your struggles have not yet caused you to be killed. ⁵You have forgotten the encouraging words that call you His children: "My child, don't think the Lord's discipline is worth nothing, and don't stop trying when He corrects you. ⁶The Lord disciplines those He loves, and He punishes everyone He accepts as His child." ⁷So hold on through your sufferings, because they are like a father's discipline. God is treating you as children. *All* children are disciplined by their fathers. ⁸If you are never

disciplined (and every child must be disciplined), you are not true children. ⁹We have all had fathers here on earth who disciplined us, and we respected them. So it is even more important that we accept discipline from the Father of our spirits so we will have life. ¹⁰Our fathers on earth disciplined us for a short time in the way they thought was best. But God disciplines us to help us, so we can become holy as he is. ¹¹We do not enjoy being disciplined. It is painful, but later, after we have learned from it, we have peace, because we start living in the right way.

So what does the Bible say is something very important that all good dads do for us? Yes, they discipline us. What does that mean, "discipline us"? It means that when we make bad choices and do the wrong thing, our dads correct us and teach us the right thing to do. At my house, when Hank and Hannah make bad choices, they get a spanking. What happens at your house when you make a bad choice? Yes, some of you get spankings, a time out, or lose the privilege of playing with your toys or watching TV.

When you do something wrong and you have a dad or mom who loves you, your parents will teach you the right way to live, and that means punishing you when you make bad choices. When Dad and Mom punish you, that means just like God, they love you so much they want you to grow up to be a holy person who respects God and other people.

It doesn't feel very good to make bad choices, and it feels even worse when we get into trouble, but when it's all over, the Bible says, we will have peace. Peace means a good feeling inside with God. Dad knows that if he punishes you when you are little for bad choices, as you grow older, you will make fewer and fewer bad choices, and it will be easier for you to obey God and honor Him with your life!

Who is thankful for spankings? That's a crazy question! Who is thankful for a dad who loves you enough to teach you how to live right and pleasing to the Lord? That's better; we all want to please God! Tell Daddy you love him and thank him for loving you even when he punishes you! Who wants to pray today?

64

Summer Vacations

Scripture: 1 Thessalonians 5:14, 18.

Christian Truth: God wants us to be patient with others always.

Visual Aid: Fun park tickets or pamphlets.

Good morning and welcome to God's house. This is the first official week of summer, and it is glorious! I love summertime!

Who is going on vacation this summer? Where are you going? Some of you are going to Disney, Dollywood, camping, and Six Flags! It is so much fun to go to the parks. What is something you have to do to get to ride on the rides? Yes! You have to stand in line. Is standing in line fun? Absolutely not—no fun whatsoever—but if you are going to ride, you have to wait your turn. Why don't we just push and shove our way around everyone and go first every time? That's right: it's rude, it's bad manners, and it doesn't make us Christlike. We don't want anyone pushing us, so we shouldn't push anyone else.

Where else do we have to wait patiently? Yes, in the checkout line, the playground, and at red lights. What about at home? Do you ever have to wait patiently? Yes, when Mom is busy—maybe talking on the phone or cooking dinner. What about when we want Mom or Dad to play with us and they are doing grown-up things?

Yes, we really must wait patiently all day, every day, everywhere.

Let's read 1 Thessalonians 5:14 and 18:

> [14] ... be patient with everyone. *(Skip down to the end of verse 18)*

> [18] ... That is what God wants for you in Christ Jesus.

The Bible says God wants us to be patient with each other. How do we wait patiently? We smile, we keep our hands to ourselves, we try to be very still, we relax, and we think about God and how it pleases Him when we wait patiently. When we are patient, we are acting like Jesus! Who wants to please God by acting like Jesus? Yes, we all do! Who wants to pray today?

Painful Boo-Boos

Scripture: Matthew 18:21–22, 35.

Christian Truth: Jesus wants us to forgive others every time.

Visual Aid: Adhesive bandages.

Good morning and welcome to God's house! How are you? It's summertime, and it's time to be outside playing all day long! Who likes to ride bikes? So much fun! Anybody ever had a wreck? It hurts so badly! Did you get cut? They really hurt. Did it hurt for a long time? What helps it stop hurting? Yes, Band-Aids help. Sometimes if it is really painful, you might have to go to the doctor. Has anyone ever broken a bone? Yes, that's really painful, and you definitely have to go to the doctor and get a cast.

After your boo-boo heals, you can take off the cast and get back on the bike again, right? Right! Just because you got hurt doesn't mean you have to stop riding your bike. Our bodies get hurt all the time on the outside, and it's sometimes really painful, but we heal and move on.

What about when we get hurt on the inside? Sometimes other people hurt our feelings, break our heart, or make us mad. What can we do to stop that pain? Can you take medicine and make it stop? No, of course not.

Let's read Matthew 18:21–22:

> ²¹Then Peter came to Jesus and asked. "Lord, when my fellow believer sins against me, how many times must I forgive him? Should I forgive him as many as seven times?" ²²Jesus answered, "I tell you, *you must forgive* him more than seven times. *You must forgive* him even if he wrongs you seventy times seven."

When other people hurt us on the inside, the only thing that takes away the pain is forgiveness. It doesn't mean what they did to you is okay; it means you are not going to live your life mad at them and hurting.

Jesus goes on to tell a story about a king who forgives a servant. The servant has an opportunity to forgive his own friend, but instead the servant puts his friend in jail for what he did to him. The king finds out and calls the servant evil for not forgiving his friend after the servant was forgiven by the king. So the king put the servant in prison too. Let's read and see what Jesus said about it.

Let's finish reading with Matthew 18:35:

> ³⁵"This king did what my heavenly Father will do to you if you do not forgive your brother or sister *from your heart.*"

That means you have to really mean it. You can't just say, "I forgive you," and not act like it. Jesus is serious about this. When you stay mad at someone, it's called bondage or like being in jail on the inside. It really feels awful to stay mad at someone. Be like Jesus and just forgive that person and forget about it!

Who wants to be free in their heart? Yes, we all do! Who wants to pray today?

Long Days of Summer

Scripture: Mark 4:37–38.

Christian Truth: God wants us to sleep well.

Visual Aid: Toothbrush and pillow.

Good morning and welcome to God's house! It's summertime, and the days are long, and you don't have to get up for school. Now that the days are longer and the sun stays up later, what do we want to do at bedtime? That's right: we want to stay up later, and the next morning we sleep later.

Why do we need to go to sleep anyway? Yes, so we will not be grouchy. Why do we get grouchy when we don't have sleep? Yes, our bodies get tired, and God made us to feel tired and grouchy so we would know our bodies need rest. Did you know that while you are sleeping, your body releases a chemical that helps you grow? Yes, it's only released when we are in cozy, deep sleep. Our bodies also release another chemical while we are sleeping that helps us heal and be healthy, but only while we are sleeping. When we go into deep sleep, God designed our body to work on our body! If we want to grow and be healthy, we need to have deep, restful sleep. Did you know when you are in deep sleep, all your organs, like your heart and brain, all rest too?

Another thing that happens while we are sleeping is learning. When we hear something new at home, school, or church during the day, our brain waits until we are sleeping to store it in our memory. So if we want to be smart, we have to get deep sleep.

What are some good habits to have at bedtime to get ready to go to sleep? Yes, eat a good healthy dinner; take a nice, warm bath; brush our teeth; get tucked in our own bed in our own room; read a Bible story; and say our prayers! Wow, if you have a regular schedule, you will be ready for good sleep.

What are some things we should do during the day to get ready for falling asleep at bedtime? Yes, after we eat lunch, we need to avoid caffeine in cola and chocolate, and all sugar in candy and desserts. These are chemicals in our food that affect our sleep. Also, stop watching TV or playing with any toys that use electricity an hour before your bedtime.

Do you think Jesus, who is God, ever was tired when He was on the earth?

Let's read Mark 4:37–38, about a time when Jesus was in a boat with his friends:

> [37]A very strong wind came up on the lake. The waves came over the sides and into the boat so that it was already full of water. [38]Jesus was at the back of the boat, sleeping with his head on a cushion.

Why do you think Jesus was sleeping? Yes, He was tired and knew His body needed rest. Who wants to be like Jesus and take care of our bodies? Yes, we all do. So we all need good sleep. When Mom or Dad says it is time for bed, I want you to hop up, say "Yes ma'am" or "Yes sir," and get busy with your bath.

Who wants to be healthy, smart, growing, and rested just like Jesus? Yes, we all do! Who wants to pray today?

Fourth of July and
the American Flag

Scripture: Psalm 33:12-13 (NIV).

Christian Truth: God promises to bless Christian nations.

Visual Aid: American flag (miniature flags to give out); US dollar bill.

Good morning and welcome to God's house. How exciting: we are celebrating the Fourth of July this week. Why do we celebrate the Fourth of July? Yes, partly because we love fireworks, but it's actually the United States of America's birthday! The Fourth of July is the day our nation was born. It is when the American colonists signed the Declaration of Independence to create the United States of America and to stop being under British rule. We fought a war against Great Britain and won our independence! So we celebrate the Fourth of July every year with cookouts, fireworks, and waving the American flag.

Did you know that a seventeen-year-old teenager named Robert G. Heft designed the American flag we have now? Pretty amazing what young people can do! Why do you think Robert put fifty stars on the flag? Yes, because there are fifty states in the United States. Robert's design was a lot like the original design from over two hundred years ago that Betsy Ross helped to create. She made the first American flag right before we signed the Declaration of Independence from the British Empire in 1776. Her flag had thirteen stars for the thirteen colonies and thirteen red and white stripes.

Benjamin Franklin is credited with suggesting that our flag should have stars to represent Heaven and because of the star that led the Wise Men to the baby Jesus in Bethlehem. Our flag has thirteen stripes for the original thirteen colonies. The red stripes are for the blood of soldiers and their bravery to protect our nation. The white stripes are for purity, which means having good moral character or making good choices that honor God. The stripes were also used to symbolize sunbeams streaming life on the earth.

What do you think blue is for? All good guesses, but the blue is for unity. That's why we are called the United States of America. To be united means to all be on the same team, all working toward the same goal.

I want you to look at this American dollar bill I have. Who wants to read what it says? Yes, it says, "In God We Trust." Godly men and women who loved Jesus and God the Father founded our nation. They wanted our nation to always put God first in our lives and to trust Him with everything. To remind us of this, they had this phrase printed on our money and all over Washington, DC, our nation's capital: "In God We Trust."

Today, however, I believe that a bunch of people in our nation are not trusting God and putting Him first in their lives. God will not bless our country if we don't put Him first. The Bible is clear that if we do not honor God with our lives, He will not bless us with protection and safety or provisions of food. On the other hand, the Bible is also very clear about what God says He will do *if* we do confess our sins and put God first.

Let's read Psalm 33:12–13 (NIV):

> [12]Blessed is the nation whose God is the Lord, the people He chose for his inheritance. [13]From heaven the Lord looks down and sees all mankind.

The Bible says that God can see every person on the earth at the same time. God can see if we are living our life to glorify Him or if we are making bad choices—called sin—that do not glorify Him. We can't trick God; He knows our heart. But we can ask God to forgive us, and He promises to forgive us. In fact, He is delighted when we ask!

If we, the people of the United States, accept Jesus as our Lord and Savior and commit our lives to Him, that means obeying God and doing what brings honor to Him. Then God promises to bless us as a nation. He promises to protect us and take care of us.

Who wants to be blessed by God this Fourth of July and every day? Me too! Who wants to pray today for our country, the United States of America? **(Pass out the miniature American flags for them to keep.)**

The Christian Flag

Scripture: Luke 14:26–27, 33.

Christian Truth: Christians represent Jesus.

Visual Aid: Miniature Christian flags to give out (available at Christian book stores and on-line).

Good morning and welcome to God's house. Last week we talked about the American flag. This week we are going to talk about another flag we have at church; we used it at Bible school. Who remembers? Yes! The Christian flag.

The Christian flag was first thought of on September 26, 1897, at Brighton Chapel in Brooklyn, New York. The Sunday school director, Charles Overton, was filling the time talking to the kids while waiting on the guest speaker, who was running late. Mr. Overton began a discussion of the American flag that was there in the room, which led him to ask the students what they thought a Christian flag should look like. They came up with lots of great ideas, and in 1907, Mr. Overton and a friend designed the first Christian flag. We still have that flag today.

What do you think the red cross is for on the Christian flag? Excellent! Yes, red is for the blood of Jesus. The red symbolizes the blood Jesus bled when He died on the cross at Calvary for our sins because He loves us. What do you think the blue is for? Blue is for Heaven, our home where we will be forever with Jesus! The blue also represents the waters of baptism. When we get saved and give our lives to Jesus, we are baptized by being dunked under water. This is a way of showing everyone that the old person is gone and we are raised up out of the water to new life in Jesus.

Look at the flag. What color do you see the most? Yes, most of it is white. What do you think the white is for on the Christian flag? It represents how, when Jesus died on the cross, He washed our sins white as snow. The white is for forgiveness. If we are God's child, all we have to do is ask Jesus and He will forgive us of all our sins. The white on the flag also stands for surrender. In battle, the soldiers that were giving up would raise a white flag. When we ask Jesus to come into our hearts as our Lord and Savior, we surrender our life to Him. We give up the way that we want to live for the way Jesus wants us to live. We no longer do what we want; instead, we do what God wants.

Let's read Luke 14:26–27 and 33:

> [26]If anyone comes to me but loves his father, mother, wife, children, brothers, or sisters—or even life—more than me, he cannot be my follower. [27]Whoever is not willing to carry the cross and follow me cannot be my follower.
>
> [33]In the same way, you must give up everything you have to be my follower.

Jesus says you must love Him first. Surrender means we give up our time and do what Jesus wants us to do. Surrender means we give up our money and spend it the way Jesus wants us to. Surrender means we live our whole life all about Jesus, telling others about Jesus and His love for us and giving God the glory for everything we do! The Christian flag tells the beautiful story of the Christian life. The Christian flag is the only flag in existence that represents people from every race, nation, and tribe. The Christian flag is a symbol of God's love for everyone. Guess what? I have a Christian flag for each of you! Who wants to pray today?

We Need Help!

Scripture: Ephesians 1:19–20.

Christian Truth: God gives us strength.

Good morning and welcome to God's house! Have you ever tried to pick something up and found it was too heavy? You have? Me too. What did you do next? Yes, we usually go get some help. What do we need to lift heavy things like big toys and chairs? Yes, we need big muscles. Muscles give us strength and make us strong! Let me see your muscles. Oh yes, they are growing bigger and bigger. The great thing about muscles is the more you use them, the bigger they get. Exercise helps our muscles grow bigger too. What if we don't use our muscles? Yes, they grow weak and aren't much use to us.

Muscles give our body strength and power, but who gives us muscles? Yes, that's right: God gives us muscles. In fact, God gives us strength for everything.

Let's read Ephesians 1:19–20:

> ¹⁹And you will know that God's power is very great for us who believe. That power is the same as his great strength ²⁰God used to raise Christ from the dead and put him at his right side in the heavenly world.

Wow! Did you hear that? If you are saved, if you have accepted Jesus as your Lord and Savior, you will have God's power inside you. Who did God give to us to live inside us? Yes, the Holy Spirit lives inside us. So we have God's power living inside us! That's so exciting! Whenever something is too hard for us to do alone, all we have to do is ask God for His power and His strength and He promises us we can do anything together with God that is for His glory. The key is *together*. We cannot do things on our own—we are too weak—but with God's power we can be strong.

Promise me not to ever give up when life is hard. Always ask God to help you, just like we ask Mom and Dad for help. God promises to always help us too! Who wants to pray today?

Getting Ready for School

Scripture: Matthew 7:12.

Christian Truth: God is honored when we share.

Visual Aid: Small boxes of crayons or pencils for each child.

Good morning and welcome to God's house. Who can tell me the name of a tool? Yes, hammers, saws, and tape measures are all great tools. Who uses those kinds of tools? Yes, a carpenter does. Who uses spatulas, big spoons, and pots and pans? Yes, a cook or chef needs different kinds of tools.

Who is starting school this week? How exciting! What kinds of tools do students need for school? Yes, you need pencils, crayons, paper, and scissors. If carpenters don't have the right tools, can they get the job done right? No, and neither can students.

Who has already been shopping and bought all their new school tools? Wow, that is everybody!

Have you been at school and seen a friend who did not have new tools for school? What could you do if you see someone in your class who does not have everything they need to get their school jobs done? Absolutely right! You could share. You can also come home and tell

78

Mom and Dad, "I would like to do some extra work around the house and buy my friend some school tools." What if you have some extra birthday money? What could you do to help? Yes, always check with your parents—but you could use that to buy your friend some school tools.

Let's read Matthew 7:12:

> [12]Do to others what you want them to do to you. This is the meaning of the Law of Moses and the teaching of the prophets.

Jesus is telling us to treat people the way we would want to be treated. If we are at school and don't have school tools we need, and someone else has some, what would we want that student to do? Yes, we would want them to share. So Jesus says that if we have something that a friend needs, we should happily share. Jesus says every time you can help someone, do it, and when you need help, someone will help you.

Today, I brought new crayons for everyone. If you don't have new crayons for school, I want you to keep this box. But if you already have new crayons for school, I want you to take this box of crayons to school and find someone who needs them and tell that person Jesus loves them! If you can't find someone to give them to, ask your teacher to help you find someone to share with, okay?

When God looks down from Heaven and sees you helping another child, what do you think God does? Yes, He smiles really big and says that's my child sharing with my other child, and that brings God honor and glory! Praise the Lord! Who wants to pray today?

Back to School

Scripture: Isaiah 49:16.

Christian Truth: We belong to God.

Good morning and welcome to God's house. Who started school this week? Oh, wow! It's so exciting! Everything is new: new shoes, new clothes, new backpacks, new school supplies, new school, new teacher, new friends, and new cubbies! What is the one thing you put on all your new stuff? Yes, you put your name on everything: your crayons, your pencil box, the place you hang your coat, and your desk. Why do we put our name on everything? That's right: to show whom it belongs to. What happens if you don't have your name on your pencil box? Yes, there can be confusion about which person it belongs to. If you put your name on the things that belong to you, no one can say it's not yours. If you buy it and put your name on it, it shows you own it—it belongs to you.

Let's read Isaiah 49:16:

> [16]See, I have written your name on my hand. Jerusalem, I always think about your walls.

Wow! Do you feel special? Our God and Creator loves us so much that He has written our names on His hand! Why do you think God did that? Yes, because we belong to Him! We are His children and He is our Heavenly Father! Just like we paid for school stuff and put our name on it to show it belongs to us, Jesus bought us with His blood when He died on the cross for our sins, and God has put our name on His hand to show we belong to Him! Our sins were purchased with the blood of Jesus. When we listen to the Holy Spirit and accept Jesus as our Savior, then we belong to God forever! Let's all shout Hallelujah! Who wants to pray today?

Bigger Than Big

Scripture: Ephesians 3:17–19.

Christian Truth: God's love is endless.

Good morning and welcome to God's house! Does anyone know how much your moms and dads love you? Yes, your parents love you a whole big bunch, don't they?

My son Hank and I play a game where we try to think up extreme amounts we can use in trying to outdo the other in telling how much we love each other. For example, I might say, "I love you more than there are grains of sand on all the beaches," and Hank might say, "I love you more than there are leaves on all the trees in the whole world!" Wow, that's a lot of love! Or we might say, "My love goes higher than the tallest trees." That's really high.

Can you think of anything taller than the tallest trees? Yes, mountains are taller, and the sky is higher than a tree. What about something really long? Yes, roads are really long. What's something longer than the longest road? Yes, the whole United States is longer, and the equator is longer than the United States. What about deeper than our Indian Boundary Lake? Yes, the ocean is deeper. What's deeper than the ocean? Can you think of anything really wide? Yes, our church is really wide. What's wider than our church? Yes, our state of Tennessee is really wide, and the whole earth is even wider.

Can you think of anything that's higher than the sky, deeper than the ocean, wider than the earth, or longer than the equator?

Let's read Ephesians 3:17–19:

> [17]I pray that Christ will live in your hearts by faith and that your life will be strong in love and built on love. [18]And I pray that you and all God's holy people will have the power to understand the greatness of Christ's love—how wide and how long and how high and how deep that love is. [19]Christ's love is greater than anyone can ever know, but I pray that you will be able to know that love. Then you can be filled with the fullness of God.

So now can you tell me what's deeper than the oceans, higher than the sky, longer than the equator, and wider than the earth? Yes! God's love is! We can't ever imagine how much God loves us or even understand it. But God loves us so much that He sent His Son Jesus to die for us! We don't have to do anything but accept God's love! Who wants to pray today?

Revenge

Scripture: Matthew 5:43–48.

Christian Truth: God is just.

Good morning and welcome to God's house! Everyone is all settled in at school. How are things going at school? Wonderful! A couple of weeks ago, we talked about how everything at school is all new. It's a new school year, with new teachers, new classrooms, new friends, and maybe some new problems.

Did anyone run into a situation where you may have had a disagreement with someone? Maybe there was a situation where someone made you mad? Yes, I have run into a few situations where I didn't agree with someone else. I thought *this* and the other person thought *that*, and we just simply didn't agree. Maybe you have run into a situation where someone at school was mean to you? Or maybe someone was making a bad choice and not sharing with you? Yes, I see heads nodding.

So what do you do in these situations when people disagree with you, make you mad, or are mean to you? We feel like being mean right back to them, don't we? Especially if someone is mean and does something like hit us—right? Wrong! We should always tell the adult in charge, and the adult will take care of it—and the person who hit us gets in trouble. If we hit back, everyone gets in trouble. What about the person who disagrees with us or the person who is making a bad choice?

Let's read Matthew 5:43–48 and see how God wants us to handle it. This is what Jesus spoke:

> [43]"You have heard that it was said 'Love your neighbor and hate your enemies.' [44]But I say to you, love your enemies. Pray for those who hurt you. [45]If you do this, you will be true children of your Father in heaven. He causes the sun to rise on good people and on evil people, and he sends rain to those who do right and to those who do wrong. [46]If you love only the people who love you, you will get no reward. Even the tax collectors do that. [47]And if you are nice only to your friends, you are no better than other people. Even those who don't know God are nice to their friends. [48]So you must be perfect, just as your Father in heaven is perfect."

So what does God want us to do with people who hurt us? Yes, forgive them and love them. That's really hard to do, but if you think about how Jesus died for us and all the bad choices we have made, then it's easier to forgive someone else and love that person like Jesus loves us. If someone is mean to us and we turn around and act mean back, then we are both mean. If someone is mean to us and we turn around and act nice toward that person, then we honor God and prove we are His children!

God promises to always take care of us, and He will—*if* we turn everything over to Him. It's hard at first, but if we will forgive the other person and show him or her God's love, we might get a chance to tell them the Good News about Jesus! Do you think someone who meets Jesus will act differently? Yes, that person will, and so should we! Who wants to pray today?

PART IV

FALL

September, October, and November

Christ's Return

Scripture: 1 Thessalonians 4:16–18.

Christian Truth: God's children know His voice.

Visual Aid: School bell.

Good morning and welcome to God's house! When you go out to the playground and you play, and then it's time to line up and come back inside, how does your teacher call you to line up? Does she or he just yell, "It's time to go!" or do they blow a whistle or maybe ring a bell? If there is more than your class on the playground and your teacher yells for you to come, how do you know when it is your teacher calling for you? That's right: you just know. You know the sound of your teacher's voice or the ring of their bell. If another teacher calls or rings a bell, do you go line up? No, because it's not the voice of your teacher. How do you know their voice so well? That's right: you know your teacher and you have heard their voice before—you know them.

It's the same way with God's voice. When you ask Jesus to come into your heart and save you, you ask Him to forgive you of your sins and ask Him to be your Lord and Savior, and then Jesus lives inside you through God's Holy Spirit! When Jesus talks to you, you know Him and you know His voice. When Jesus calls you to be saved, you can hear His voice. When we are saved, we can hear God's voice talking to us.

When we die, where are we going to live with Jesus? Yes! Heaven is where Jesus is now and where we will live forever with Jesus!

What if Jesus comes back to earth to get His church before we die—how will we know Jesus has come back for us?

Let's read 1 Thessalonians 4:16–18:

> [16]The Lord himself will come down from heaven with a loud command, with the voice of the archangel, and with the trumpet call of God. And those who have died believing in Christ will rise first. [17]After that, we who are still alive will be gathered up with them in the clouds to meet the Lord in the air. And we will be with the Lord forever. [18]So encourage each other with these words.

So how will we know Jesus has come back for us? Yes, we will hear His voice and we will know it's time to go! Praise to God! Who wants to pray today?

Sin

Scripture: Luke 19:10.

Christian Truth: Jesus came to save all people from their sins.

Visual Aid: Backpack or pencil.

Good morning and welcome to God's house! Have you ever lost something like your backpack, a pencil, or maybe your shoe? Everyone does occasionally. I lose my car keys all the time.

What does it mean when something's lost? Yes, it means it's missing, or gone, but you don't have it. You are separated from it. What does it mean when we say you are separated from it? Yes, it means you're not together; you're not connected to it. What does it mean to be separated from God? It means the same thing. It means we are not together. We are not connected.

What's the only thing that separates us from God? Very good! Yes, sin separates us from God. According to the Bible, everyone is born a sinner. We are born lost from God. We are born separated from God.

How can we be connected to God or in a relationship with God? Yes, Jesus knew we are sinners. God will only allow perfect holiness in His presence. But we are not perfect and holy because we sin, so that means we would not be able to go to Heaven and live with God when we die. So we find ourselves in a mess. The Bible says we can't fix this mess ourselves, but guess who can fix it and did fix it?

Let's read Luke 19:10:

> [10]The Son of Man came to find lost people and save them.

So Jesus volunteered to leave Heaven, come die on the cross for us, and take all our sins on His body, to make us holy and without sin in God's eyes. When we ask Jesus to forgive us of our sins and ask Him to be the Lord of our life, He saves us! Then when God looks at us, He doesn't see us as the old sinner—He sees us as the new child born again through Christ!

This allows us to be connected to God. We aren't lost anymore! We are saved! We are God's children forever! We can't ever be lost again or separated from God! Praise the Lord! Who wants to pray today?

Making Good Choices

Scripture: Galatians 5:22–23.

Christian Truth: Christians need self-control.

Visual Aid: Grade card.

Good morning and welcome to God's house! Everyone's all settled in school, and you have already gotten a three-week progress report. Wow, time flies by quickly! What is a progress report? That's right: it's a report to Mom and Dad about how hard you are working at school. If you work really hard, you get what? Yes, you get an A, and if you aren't working hard at all, what do you get? Yes, you get a D or an F! Oh my, that would mean some big improvement was necessary! So the progress report or grade card tells how well you're doing.

What if Mom and Dad gave you a grade card for how well you are doing at home and you had to bring it to church to show Pastor Rick? Would you get an A in every area for working hard and doing well at home? Well, we've got a few telling the truth and saying they might have a C now and then.

What if God gave us a report card for how well we were doing as Christians? How do you think you would do? What do you think would be on God's grade card? Yes, definitely the Ten Commandments.

What else? How about the fruits of the Spirit? Yes, I think how well we are loving, giving, and being patient would definitely be on there.

There is another fruit that would be on there as well. Maybe you know this fruit or behavior that God talks about. It is the fruit of making the right choice- when we really want to make a bad choice because it's what we want and not what God wants.

Let's read Galatians 5:22–23. Listen carefully and see if you can find it:

> 22But the Spirit produces the fruit of love, joy, peace, patience, kindness, goodness, faithfulness, 23gentleness, **self-control**. There is no law that says these things are wrong.

Yes, God says we must have self-control. Many times, we want to do something, and we know it is a bad choice or something we shouldn't do, but we want to do it really badly. When we listen to the Holy Spirit and we do what He guides us to do, He will lead us to make a good choice every time and bring God glory! When we honor God with our effort and choices, we are using self-control. We are being obedient to the Holy Spirit! It feels good to make the right choice. When we choose to work hard and follow the Holy Spirit's directions—the first time—we make the right choice every time and we have self-control!

Who is going to listen to the Holy Spirit when He speaks to you? Yes, that will bring God glory! Who wants to pray today?

Me, Myself, and I

Scripture: Luke 10:27-28.

Christian Truth: The key to loving others is to love and respect ourselves.

Visual Aid: Mirror.

Good morning and welcome to God's house! Who are you with all the time? Yes, you are with Mom and Dad a lot, and Grandma and Grandpa, but who are you with twenty-four hours a day, every second? Yes, you are with *you* every second, every minute, every hour—all day, every day. You talk to yourself more than anyone else. You figure things out by yourself. You may be with different people in your family at different times, but ultimately, you are with you all the time!

Do you like yourself? Do you love yourself? Of course you do. How about when you mess up or make a bad choice or a bad decision? We don't usually like ourselves very much at those times.

What about loving other people? It's easy to love others when they do what we want, but what about when they don't do what we want? Yes, it's much harder, isn't it?

Let's read Luke 10:27-28, about a conversation Jesus had with a man:

> 27The man answered, "Love the Lord your God with all your
> heart, all your soul, all your strength, and all your mind."
> Also, "Love your neighbor as you love yourself." 28Jesus said
> to him, "Your answer is right. Do this and you will live."

Jesus says for us to love others the way we love ourselves. You can't love others if you don't love yourself. Loving others starts with loving yourself.

What are some ways we can love ourselves? We can respect ourselves by saying nice things about ourselves; never call yourself a bad name or put yourself down. We need to talk nicely about ourselves, even when we mess up—then we will talk nicely about others when they mess up.

What about forgiving ourselves when we make mistakes? Yes, Jesus died to forgive us for our sins, so when we mess up or sin, we need to ask God to forgive us, and if we are serious, He will forgive us. We also need to forgive ourselves—make up our minds to make better choices that honor God, and move on past it. If we learn to forgive ourselves when we mess up, then we will learn to forgive others when they mess up too.

What about accepting ourselves the way we are as a way to love ourselves? Yes, we need to accept that God created us just the way He wanted: some of us are tall; some are short; some have blue eyes; some have brown or hazel; and some of us have blond hair or black or brown. When we understand God made us just the way He wanted, then we can love ourselves just the way He made us!

How can we love our bodies (which are the temple of the Holy Spirit) and our brains? Yes, we can take care of our bodies and our brains! We can exercise every day, eat healthy foods, and get good sleep every night. Yes, when we respect ourselves, we will love and respect others as well.

Who wants to honor God and love others by the way we love ourselves? Yes, let's only say nice words to ourselves; let's forgive ourselves when we make a bad choice or sin; and let's accept our bodies and brains as God's perfect creation by the way we take care of ourselves. This will lead to respecting other people as well. Who wants to pray today?

Autumn

Scripture: Psalm 150:1–6.

Christian Truth: Everything in nature tells about and praises the sacrifice of Jesus Christ.

Good morning and welcome to God's house. Wow, the weather is changing so quickly, and we are moving into a new season! It was summertime, but now what season is it? Yes, it's turning into fall or autumn. That means jackets, football, hot chocolate, and the leaves start turning colors!

What happens to the leaves after they turn colors? Yes, they die and fall off the tree. Why does this happen? The leaves make something called chlorophyll, which they use to catch sunshine and make food and energy for the tree to grow. In the fall, the trees stop growing so the tree can rest, and the leaves stop making chlorophyll because the tree doesn't need the extra food for growing. The chlorophyll in the leaves is what makes the leaves appear to be green. Actually, green leaves have other colors we can't see while they are making chlorophyll. When the leaves stop making chlorophyll, the other colors can be seen temporarily then the leaves die. The leaves fall off the tree because the tree doesn't need leaves for a while. The leaves have served their purpose, so they die.

Everything in nature tells the story of Christ's life here on earth, especially the seasons. Spring is when everything is new and the animals have their babies. All the babies being born in spring reminds me of when Christ was born on the earth as a little baby.

Then comes summertime—that's when all the earth is working so hard to produce crops, and it's alive and growing. That is just like when Jesus walked on the earth. When Jesus began His ministry to preach the Good News of God's love, He worked and worked to tell everyone so that they could be saved. Remember, He said the harvest is great. He was talking about all the people that didn't know about God's love and needed Jesus to be saved.

What season is after summer? Yes, that would be fall, where we are now. Fall is when everything stops growing, the leaves all die, and that reminds us of when Jesus stopped preaching and when He died on the cross for our sins. Just like the leaves die when they have served their purpose, Jesus came to die for us—that was His purpose.

What season is next? Yes, winter comes next, and winter is when everything rests and sleeps. The animals all sleep, and the new baby leaves are growing inside the buds while the tree sleeps through three months of winter. This reminds me of Jesus lying in the tomb for three days!

Then comes spring, and just like the new leaves burst out of the buds, so did Jesus burst out of the tomb! The angels announced, "He is risen!" Who does the Bible say created the earth and everything in it? Yes, God created all things, and the Bible says God created all things for His Son Jesus. It's amazing to discover all the ways that everything in creation tells the story of Christ's love for us!

Let's read Psalm 150:

> [1]Praise the Lord! Praise God in His Temple; praise him in His mighty heaven. [2]Praise him for his strength; praise him

for his greatness. ³Praise him with trumpet blasts; praise him with harps and lyres. ⁴Praise him with tambourines and dancing; praise him with stringed instruments and flutes. ⁵Praise him with loud cymbals; praise him with crashing cymbals. ⁶Let everything that breathes praise the Lord. Praise the Lord!

Wow! That makes me want to shout and praise the Lord! The Bible says for *everything* that's breathing to praise the Lord. Everyone take a deep breath. If you are alive, you are breathing. What does the Bible say for everything that's breathing to do? Yes, just like all of creation, we are to praise the Lord!

What are some ways to praise the Lord? Yes, we can play instruments; we can sing; we can shout; we can lift our hands; and we can tell other people about God's love and how Jesus died for everyone! We can help feed hungry people, give them clothes, give them a place to live, help them when they are sick, and visit them in jail or prison. Yes, there are many ways to praise the Lord using our brains, mouths, hands, and feet!

The most important thing is to not be afraid. Just do it! On the count of three, let's all lift our hands together and say, "Praise the Lord!" Ready, 1–2–3, Praise the Lord! Who wants to pray today?

Jack-O-Lanterns

Scripture: Matthew 5:14–16; 6:22.

Christian Truth: Christians are to be God's light to all people.

Visual Aid: Flashlight.

Good morning and welcome to God's house! How are you? Wonderful! I am so excited—we carved our pumpkin last night, and it was so much fun! Who is carving a pumpkin at your house? Are you making a scary face or fun face? Yes, we made a fun, happy face.

While we were carving our pumpkin, it occurred to me that Christians are just like jack-o-lanterns! What is the first thing you have to do if you want a jack-o-lantern? Yes, you have to go pick out a pumpkin, either at the pumpkin farm or at the market. That started me thinking: that's what God does with us. He picks us to be His children. When we are becoming saved, we first hear God's voice calling us to Him. God chooses us!

After you pick your pumpkin, then what do you do with it? Well, if you get it at the farm, you have to wash it and clean it up; it's usually got dirt on it from the field. That's the same with us when we get saved. We are covered with dirty sin, and God cleans us up. When Jesus died on the cross, He died for all our sins forever. We were sinners, but the Bible says Jesus washes us white as snow!

What's next in creating a jack-o-lantern? Yes, you have to reach inside and scoop out the pulp and seeds. Jesus does the same with us when He saves us. He reaches inside us and scoops out all the junk we are carrying around inside us that we don't need. He scoops out the seeds of doubt, greed, hate, and fear.

What do we do next to our pumpkin to turn it into a jack-o-lantern? Yes, we put a big smile on it just like Jesus does for us when He saves us. What's the last thing we do to our jack-o-lantern? Yes, we put a light inside it.

Let's read Matthew 5:14–16 and 6:22:

> [14]You are the light that gives light to the world. A city that is built on a hill cannot be hidden. [15]And people don't hide a light under a bowl. They put it on a lampstand so the light shines for all the people in the house. [16]In the same way, you should be a light for other people. Live so that they will see the good things you do and will praise your Father in heaven.
>
> [22]The eye is the light for the body. If your eyes are good, your whole body will be full of light.

Jesus fills us with His light *(turn on the flashlight)*, which is the Holy Spirit, when He saves us—just like when you put a candle inside the jack-o-lantern. The light fills it up. Jesus fills us up with His light, which is His love for others to see. We are to live in a way that other people who do not know Jesus will see Jesus in us and want to know Jesus too! We can't do what we want; we must do what Jesus wants, and that will make us shine God's light to the entire world!

Who wants to shine their light of God's love on others? We all do! Who wants to pray today?

Growing Pumpkins

Scripture: Philippians 1:6.

Christian Truth: As disciples of Jesus Christ, we spend our whole life learning about Jesus to grow closer to our Lord and to be apostles or messengers for Christ.

Visual Aid: Pumpkin.

Good morning and welcome to God's house! Who has pumpkins at their house? Yes, I love to decorate with pumpkins in the fall. Who has carved their jack-o-lantern? Where do jack-o-lanterns come from? Yes, they come from pumpkins. Where do pumpkins come from? Yes, you are all so smart—pumpkins come from seeds. Where do pumpkin seeds come from? Yes, they come from pumpkins. If you have pumpkin seeds, how do you get them to turn into pumpkins? That's right: you have to plant them. Where do you plant them—in the sandbox? No, that's silly; you plant them in the soil, where they can get vitamins and minerals.

What else does a pumpkin need to grow? Yes, to grow, it needs sunshine, space, water, and air. Can you leave out some of the things the pumpkin needs and still grow a pumpkin? No, God designed it that way for all plants to grow. Can you rush it? No, it takes about one hundred days to grow a pumpkin, and you can't rush it. The baby seed needs time to grow; and then the little sprout pops out; and then the stem grows up and the leaves pop out; and finally, there is a blossom with a baby pumpkin inside!

After it grows into a mature pumpkin, you can do all kinds of things with it. You can cook a pie, use it as a decoration, make a jack-o-lantern, or even grow more pumpkins! Christians are the same way. When we accept Jesus as our Lord and Savior, we start to grow and grow as Christians, just like the pumpkin seed. Just like the growing pumpkin, Christians must have certain things designed by God to help us grow. We need Sunday school and daily Bible study, as well as worship, prayer time in a secret place with just us and God, and fellowship with other Christians. We also need to be obedient to God's voice and confess our sins to God when we sin and stop doing that sin.

Can you think of other ways we learn about Jesus and grow in our relationship with Him? Yes, by coming to Bible school, Team Kid on Wednesday nights, and revival. Do we need to learn about Jesus every day? Yes! What if we only watered our pumpkin some of the time and gave it sunshine some of the time? Yes, it would eventually die. Christians are the same way spiritually; we need to feed our souls with learning as much as we can every day about Jesus.

Just like the pumpkins, when we grow as Christians, God can use us in different ways. Some of you will grow up and become singers for God, some of you will be preachers and teachers, and some of you will be local or foreign missionaries! How exciting! It takes about one hundred days for a pumpkin seed to grow into a mature pumpkin. How long do you think it takes to grow into a mature Christian?

Let's read Philippians 1:6:

> ⁶"God began doing a good work in you, and I am sure he will continue it until it is finished when Jesus Christ comes again.

The Bible says that God wants us to continue learning about Jesus until Jesus comes back to earth to get us. We are called to be disciples of Jesus every day of our whole life! Who wants to learn about Jesus every day? Yes, me too! Who wants to pray today?

Trick or Treat

Scripture: Hebrews 4:12–13.

Christian Truth: We can't hide anything from God.

Visual Aid: Halloween mask.

Good morning and welcome to the house of God! Who is trick-or-treating for Halloween? It is very important to always remember to only go to the houses of people who we know, like family and friends, and it's really important to only go with your parents or another family member, right?

What are you dressing up as? Why do we dress up in costumes? Yes, it's fun, and when we disguise ourselves under a costume, we can fool or trick people and they don't know who it is! Who is going to wear a mask? That's an even better way to disguise yourself. If you have on a costume and a mask, it's going to be really hard for anyone to know who you are, right? Who will probably know who you are? Yes, Mom and Dad, because they help you put your costume together, and they help you get ready.

But who else knows who's hidden behind your costume? That's right: God does! God knows everything! God even knows what we are thinking. God knows when we tell the truth and when we tell a lie.

God knows when you are nice and kind to others and when you aren't. God knows if we steal or if we say things we shouldn't. Even if no one else sees what we do, or no one else knows what we are feeling or thinking—even if we think it's a secret from everyone, including Mom and Dad—God knows everything we do and say!

Can we trick God? No, not ever! We can trick ourselves and think God doesn't know what we are doing, but He always knows everything.

Let's read Hebrews 4:12–13:

> [12]God's word is alive and working and is sharper than a double-edged sword. It cuts all the way into us, where the soul and the spirit are joined, to the center of our joints and bones. And it judges the thoughts and feelings in our hearts. [13]Nothing in all the world can be hidden from God. Everything is clear and lies open before him, and to Him we must explain the way we have lived.

Dressing up and trick-or-treating is so much fun. But as a Christian, can we ever trick God? No, the Bible is very clear: God knows everything, and one day, the Bible says, everyone will have to bow before God and explain why we did the things we did, good or bad, and why we lived the way we did! Who wants to be ashamed of the way we lived when they face God? No one does! Who wants to live their life in a way to honor God? Yes, we all do! Who wants to pray today?

The Fullness of the Earth

Scripture: Colossians 1:16.

Christian Truth: God made everything.

Visual Aid: Apple to show; basket of apples to give to the children.

Good morning and welcome to God's house. How are all of you? It's fall and it's cool weather and apple time! Who loves apples? I love apples! What's your favorite way to eat apples? I love plain apples, and my son delights in applesauce. Yes, there are caramel apples, apple pie, and dried apples. Where do we get apples? Yes, the store, but where do they get them? Yes, the farmer, but where does the farmer get them? Yes, the apple tree, but where does the apple tree get them? Yes, from apple seeds, and where do the apple seeds come from? Yes, from the apples—and it starts all over again. Who made the first apples with the first seeds? Yes, God made them! In fact, God made everything we have.

Let's read Colossians 1:16:

> [16]Through His power [God's power] all things were made—
> things in heaven and on earth, things seen and unseen, all
> powers, authorities, lords and rulers. All things were made
> through Christ and for Christ.

God is an awesome God! He made it all. Anything you can think of—God made it! And He made it all for Jesus, His Son, and God allows us, his children, to live among his creation and enjoy it. God made the sun, moon, and stars; the ocean; the air we breathe; and even us! When we pray, what can we tell God for making us and everything we see and can't see? Yes, we need to say, "Thank you, God!" Let's pray right now and thank God for creating us and everything in the whole world! Who wants to pray today?

I Am Unique

Scripture: Psalm 139:13–16.

Christian Truth: God made me special.

Visual Aid: Crayons—red, tan, black, blue, gray, brown, yellow, and green.

Good morning and welcome to God's house! How are you? It's wonderful to have all of you here to worship our Lord and Savior Jesus Christ! Who likes to draw pictures? When you draw a picture and you forget to put your name on it and someone says it's his or her picture, what do you say? Yes, you say it's mine, because I know what I made and I know what colors I used. You can describe your creation because you made it, and that proves it belongs to you.

Let's play a game: when I hold up a crayon, raise your hand if you have that color of hair. Who has red hair? Black hair? Brown hair? Gray hair? Who has blue eyes? Brown eyes? Green eyes? Or blue-green, called hazel eyes? Who has skin that is a shade of red? A shade of yellow? A shade of black? A shade of tan?

Wow, we all have special shades and combinations of color! Who made us beautiful like a rainbow? Yes, God made us all and made us just the way He wanted!

Let's read Psalm 139:13–16:

> ¹³You made my whole being; you formed me in my mother's body. ¹⁴I praise you because you made me in an amazing and wonderful way. What you have done is wonderful. I know this very well. ¹⁵You saw my bones being formed as I took shape in my mother's body. When I was put together there, ¹⁶you saw my body as it was formed. All the days planned for me were written in your book before I was one day old.

Did you know that since the beginning with the first people, Adam and Eve, there has never been another you! You are so special! God made only one of you! And forever, there will be only one of you!

Why do you think God created us so special? Yes, because He has a special, unique love for each of us and a special, unique purpose for each of us! It is just like when the red crayon makes red when you draw, and the blue crayon makes blue, and when we put all the special colors together, we get a beautiful picture! What if all the crayons were the same color; what if instead of twenty-four different shades of color, we had twenty-four of just one color? That would be pretty boring!

God created us to be special too. We do not have to be just like everyone else. We can be who God wants us to be. God is our Heavenly Father, and He loves us personally. That means He wants to have a personal relationship with each of us!

Always tell God thank you for the way He created us, and say thank you that we belong to God as His unique, one-of-a-kind child! Who wants to pray today?

Thanksgiving Day

Scripture: Philippians 4:4–7.

Christian Truth: God's children are to come before God with thankfulness to God.

Good morning and welcome to God's house. This week we celebrate a big holiday. That's right: it's Thanksgiving Day. What is Thanksgiving Day? Yes, it's where we eat turkey with our family and watch football. Is that all? Who knows how Thanksgiving started? Yes, hundreds of years ago, a group of people across the Atlantic Ocean lived in a kingdom where the king decided how they would worship, where they worshipped and who they worshipped, and the people were unhappy with this system. So they decided to leave and sail across the ocean to a newly discovered place called America and start a new life there and make their own rules about worship.

Do you know the name of the people who came to America? Yes, they were called Pilgrims, and they sailed on a famous ship called the Mayflower. Well, when they arrived in America, they cut down trees and started building houses and looking for food. Why didn't they just run to the store? That's right: there were no stores. There wasn't anything but land and the Wampanoag Native Americans or Indians.

Well, winter came, and it became even harder for the Pilgrims. They didn't have enough food, and a bunch of them got sick. There weren't any doctors or medicine, and many of the Pilgrims died. The Wampanoag Indians felt sorry for the Pilgrims and came and brought them food. They showed them how to hunt and fish for food. That spring, the Indians shared seeds with the Pilgrims and helped the Pilgrims plant gardens so they would be ready for the next winter. All summer they worked in the garden, and when fall came, they harvested their crops; that means they got all the food out of the garden and saved it for winter to eat.

The Pilgrims were so thankful to God for sending the Indians to help them, and they were so thankful for all the food God had grown for them, that they decided to have a feast and celebrate. That was in the year 1621. The Pilgrims invited the Indians, said a blessing over the food, and thanked God for saving their lives and for sending the Indians to help teach them how to survive in America. The Pilgrims were so thankful, and celebrated the first Thanksgiving Day by praising and worshiping God.

We have been celebrating Thanksgiving Day for almost four hundred years! Our first president of the United States, George Washington, proclaimed the first nationwide Thanksgiving Day in the United States on Thursday, November 26, 1789. He said it was a day of public thanksgiving and prayer to Almighty God.

Later, in 1863, a woman named Sarah Hale had been writing letters to each president of the United States for forty years, asking that Thanksgiving be celebrated on the same day every year to create unity in the United States. So President Abraham Lincoln proclaimed the final Thursday in November as our national day of thanksgiving and prayer to God. In 1941, President Franklin D. Roosevelt signed federal legislation that made Thanksgiving Day a national holiday on the fourth Thursday of November.

Why do you think our Founding Fathers and presidents of the United States, all through our history, have made sure we have Thanksgiving Day?

Let's read Philippians 4:4–7:

> ⁴Be full of joy in the Lord always. I will say again, be full of joy. ⁵Let everyone see that you are gentle and kind. The Lord is coming soon. ⁶Do not worry about anything, but pray and ask God for everything you need, always giving thanks. ⁷And God's peace, which is so great we cannot understand it, will keep your hearts and minds in Christ Jesus.

So according to the Bible, why did our Founding Fathers and our presidents all throughout our history think Thanksgiving Day was so important? Yes, because the Bible teaches us to tell God thank you. We need to acknowledge that Almighty God is the one true God and we are His children. We need to tell God we know that everything we have comes from Him. What does the Bible say God will give us if we are thankful? Yes, He will give us His peace and keep us close to Jesus!

Who thinks that Thanksgiving Day and being thankful to God are important? Yes, I do too! Who wants to pray right now and tell God we are thankful He is our loving Heavenly Father and we need Him to watch over us and protect us, take care of us, and forgive us? Okay, who wants to pray?

Who Knows?

Scripture: Psalm 147:4–5.

Christian Truth: God knows everything.

Visual Aid: Clear glass full of sand.

Good morning and welcome to God's house! How are you? Wonderful. Let me ask you a question: who do you know that is really smart? Yes, moms, dads, mamaws, and papaws are all really smart. They know a lot of stuff. Do you know someone who knows everything? Yes, moms are smart, and they know the answer to just about everything humans can know—or at least the important things. But who is the only person who knows everything about everything?

I have a glass full of sand; how many grains of sand do you think are in my glass? It would be impossible to count. If we had one thousand people count each grain of sand, everyone would come up with a different number—even moms!

Who knows how many blades of grass there are on the whole earth or how many leaves on the trees? What about how many waves are on the ocean or how many stars are in the sky?

Let's read Psalm 147:4–5:

> ⁴He counts the stars and names each one. ⁵Our Lord is great and very powerful. There is no limit to what he knows.

So who knows everything? Yes, God our Heavenly Father knows everything. He even knows everything about you! Look at your friend sitting beside you. God knows even how many hairs are on your head! Our Heavenly Father is a *big* God! We can't even understand how great and how big our God is. And guess what? He loves you with all His power, majesty, and might! We are His children, and He is our God!

The next time you have a problem you can't figure out, don't tell God how big your problem is—tell your problem how big our God is! Will you promise to do that? Wonderful! Who wants to pray to God today?

PART V

Extra Lessons for Months with Five Sundays

God's Holy Spirit

Scripture: Psalm 90:13–14.

Christian Truth: God's love lives inside us through the Holy Spirit.

Who likes to play in the sandbox? It's so much fun, and you can make sand castles. What do you need to make sand castles? What if you have sand buckets but no sand? Can you still build sand castles? No. What if you have sand buckets and sand, but you only fill them half full? That will not work either. If you want to make a great sand castle, you have to fill the bucket all the way full with sand. What are some other things we can fill up? Yes, a glass with chocolate milk, swimming pools, shoeboxes with toys for other kids, and closets with clothes. What about us? Can we fill ourselves up? Yes, we can fill our tummies with food, but that just fills our tummies. What can fill us up from the top of our head to the tips of our toes?

Let's read Psalm 90:13–14:

> ¹³Lord, how long before you return and show kindness to your servants? ¹⁴Fill us with your love every morning; Then we will sing and rejoice all our lives.

Isn't that awesome! We can ask God every morning to fill us head to toe with His love! What is God's love? In 1 Corinthians 13, the Bible says God's love is patience, kindness—not bragging on ourselves or acting rude. God's love isn't selfish and always tells the truth. Wow, can you imagine if we ask God to fill us up head to toe every morning with all that?

Who does God use to put His love inside us? Yes, the Holy Spirit of God brings His love. Do you think that if we started every day filled with the power of God's love, it would change the way our day goes and everyone else's day too? Yes, it would!

When you wake up every morning, can you ask God to fill you up head to toe with His love? Will you watch to see how being filled with God's love changes everything about your life? Wonderful! Who wants to pray today?

Making a Difference

Scripture: 2 Corinthians 8:19.

Christian Truth: God wants His children to sincerely care for others.

Visual Aid: A starfish.

Good morning and welcome to God's house! I want to tell you a story today.

> Early one morning there was an old man walking on the beach when he saw a young boy and girl bending over and throwing something gently into the ocean. He asked them, "What are you doing?"
>
> The young boy replied, "Throwing starfish into the ocean."
>
> "Why?" asked the startled old man.
>
> The young girl answered, "The sun is up, and the tide is going out. If we don't help throw them back in the water, they will die."
>
> Upon hearing this, the wise man pointed to the miles and miles of beach covered with starfish and said to the young

people, "Do you not realize how many starfish there are? You can't possibly make a difference!"

The young boy bent down, picked up another starfish, and gently threw it in the ocean. As it slipped into the ocean, the boy said, "It made a difference to that one!"

The old man looked at the young people and thought about what they said. Inspired, the old man joined the boy and girl and started picking up the starfish and gently throwing them back into the ocean. Soon other people came and started to help, and the beach looked very different that day.

Why do you think the young girl and boy were helping the starfish? Yes, because they loved the starfish. Love comes from God, and God wants us to be loving. In what way could we share God's love with others? Yes, by helping others in need, just like the boy and girl were helping. Can we help everyone in the whole world in one day? No, but everyday we can help someone. Every day, God gives us a divine appointment to help someone. We just need to focus on the person we are to help today. Did you know that when we help someone in need, we are sharing the love of God inside us with the other person?

Let's read 2 Corinthians 8:19:

> … we are doing this service to bring glory to the Lord and to show that we really want to help.

God gives us divine appointments or "God appointments" with people who need to feel God's love. God includes us, and it's exciting and wonderful. Many people don't even know God or understand that God loves them. When we help people, we get to share God's love with them, help them, and tell them about Jesus! The Bible also says that when we share God's love by helping others, we bring glory to our Lord Jesus, and that gives glory to our Heavenly Father! Can you watch for an opportunity every day to help someone and show that person you really care about him or her? Wonderful! Who wants to pray today?

Whose Truth?

Scripture: John 14:6.

Christian Truth: God's Word is our truth.

Good morning and welcome to God's house! Who knows what the truth is? I hear some of you asking, "The truth about what?" What is truth about anything? What does it mean to tell the truth? Yes, it means to tell what really happened.

Have you ever been in a situation where someone asked what happened and you told what you saw happen, and someone else told what he or she thought happened, and both stories were completely different? One person told the truth and the other person did what? Yes, the other person told a lie.

Who decides who is telling the truth and who is lying or not telling the truth? Yes, God does, according to His Word. Can we just say, "Well, that's my truth and my way," and that will be okay with God? No, absolutely not. When we believe we can decide what's okay for us and live however we want, who are we lying to then? Yes, we are lying to ourselves. We have to decide who we are going to follow in life. Are we going to go our own way and live our life however we want to, or are we going to accept God's truth and God's ways as our truth?

Let's read John 14:6:

> ⁶Jesus answered, "I am the way, and the truth, and the life. The only way to the Father is through me."

The Bible is crystal clear: Jesus is the only truth. We cannot live our life any way we want and still expect to get to God, our Creator, in Heaven. Jesus is clear that He is the only way. The Bible is God's Word. The Bible is our truth to follow through life and to Heaven. When you accept Jesus as your Savior, God gives us His Holy Spirit to live in us to guide us and show us the truths of God and the right way to live according to God.

When we live according to God's Holy Bible, whom do we honor? Yes, we honor God with our life. When we go our own way and live according to the way we want, whom do we honor? Yes, we honor the devil!

Who wants to live their life according to what the Bible says and bring glory to our Heavenly Father? Yes! Me too! How are we going to know all the truths in the Bible? Yes, we have to read it, listen when Mom and Dad read to us, and listen to our teachers and Pastor Rick! The more we hear God's Word, the more we will know God's truth.

When we read the Bible and learn how God wants us to live, what should we do? Yes, follow God's truth and make the right choices according to the Bible! Who wants to pray today?

Names

Scripture: Deuteronomy 5:11.

Christian Truth: God's name is holy.

Good morning and welcome to God's house! Who knows their whole name—first, middle, and last? Wow! All beautiful names! Anyone named after someone? Wonderful! I named my daughter Hannah Ruth after my sister Ruth and my mom's sister, my Aunt Ruth. That makes her name extraspecial!

Have you ever had anyone make fun of your name? Yes, and it hurts, doesn't it? It's just mean and disrespectful. What does disrespectful mean? It means not showing respect for the other person or not caring about how the other person feels.

What about God's name? When we say God's name, how should we use it? Yes, we should say God's name with respect when we are praying, telling others about Him, or reading the Bible out loud. What about saying God's name out loud when we are mad? No, that would be disrespectful. What about just saying God's name when we are excited or scared but we aren't talking to God at all? No, that's very disrespectful also, isn't it?

Let's read Deuteronomy 5:11:

> ¹¹You must not use the name of the Lord your God thoughtlessly, because the Lord **will punish** anyone who uses His name in this way.

According to the Bible, do you think God is serious about using His name with disrespect? Yes, God says He will punish anyone—that includes everyone, doesn't it? God is holy, and He deserves respect from His children. Who has ever been punished at home when you made a bad choice? Thank you for telling the truth. I was punished when I was little when I made a bad choice too. I usually got a spanking and it hurt! When you get punished, does it hurt? Of course it does. Do you think that if we use God's name disrespectfully, He will do what he says and punish us? Yes, I am sure of it. Who likes to get in trouble and get punished? No one does, so let's be smart and respectful to God.

Let's show our Father God how much we do love and care about Him! When we talk to other people, let's only say God's name in a loving, respectful way, because God is holy! Who wants to pray to God today?

CPSIA information can be obtained at www.ICGtesting.com
Printed in the USA
LVOW09s1557141014

408703LV00003B/691/P